DARK VOYAGER

A play

by

John Misto

FOR ALL ENQUIRIES CONTACT: ORiGiN™ Theatrical
PO BOX Q1235, QVB Post Office, Sydney, NSW, 1230, Australia
Phone: (61 2) 8514 5201 Fax: (61 2) 9299 2920
enquiries@originmusic.com.au   www.origintheatrical.com.au
Part of the ORiGiN™ Music Group
An Australian Independent Music Company

1

IMPORTANT NOTICE

should not be considered to be necessarily endorsing or otherwise attempting to promote an affiliation with any of the owners of the brand names or trademarks or public figures. Such references are solely for use in a dramatic context.

LANGUAGE NOTE

Licensees are welcome to make small alterations to the language that is used is this play so as to make it suitable for a younger cast and/or audience.

MUSIC USE NOTE

Licensees are solely responsible for obtaining formal written permission from copyright owners to use copyrighted music in the performance of this play and are strongly cautioned to do so. If no such permission is obtained by the licensee, then the licensee must use only original music that the licensee owns and controls. Licensees are solely responsible and liable for all music clearances and shall indemnify the copyright owners of the play(s) and their licensing agent, ORiGiN™ Theatrical, against any costs, expenses, losses and liabilities arising from the use of music by licensees. Please contact the appropriate music licensing authority in your territory for the rights to any incidental music. In Australia and New Zealand, contact APRA AMCOS apraamcos.com.au.

If you are in any doubt about any of the above then contact ORiGiN™ Theatrical.

For complete listing of plays and musicals available to perform and all licence enquiries, contact ORiGiN™ Theatrical.

www.origintheatrical.com.au
+ 61 2 8514 5201

AND HERE ARE THE RULES
IN PLAIN ENGLISH FOR YOU...

<u>DO NOT</u> perform this play without getting permission from ORiGiN™ Theatrical first. In 99% of cases you'll need to pay us money to be allowed to stage a performance. This money goes to the author(s) of the show who shed blood, sweat and tears creating this play. Please don't rob them of their livelihood.
Go online www.origintheatrical.com.au or call +61 2 8514 5201

<u>DO NOT</u> make a copy of this book by photocopying, scanning, taking a photo, retyping (on a computer or a typewriter), or using a pencil, pen or chalkboard. If you want to purchase more copies contact ORiGiN™ Theatrical.
Go online www.origintheatrical.com.au or call +61 2 8514 5201

<u>DO NOT</u> make any changes to the text without first getting permission from ORiGiN™ Theatrical in writing. Sometimes you'll be allowed to make changes and sometimes you won't. Please always check with us first.
Go online www.origintheatrical.com.au or call +61 2 8514 5201

<u>DO NOT</u> record your performances or rehearsals in any way without first getting permission from ORiGiN™ Theatrical. We know everyone wants to try and record everything on their phones these days. We get it. But please don't encourage them or give them permission. Sometimes there are important contractual reasons as to why we can't give you permission to record it. And sometimes there aren't any reasons and we can say YES. Please just check with us first.
Go online www.origintheatrical.com.au or call +61 2 8514 5201

<u>DO</u> contact ORiGiN™ Theatrical if you have any questions about anything. At all. And we mean anything. One of us that works here (not me) has a peculiar interest in recording the unusual bird calls of the adult hoatzin (a species of tropical bird found in wet forest and mangrove of the Amazon and the Orinoco delta in South America) so we should be able to answer any questions you have about the Hoatzin. Plus we know some things about some other things too.

Thank you for taking the time to read this.

ABOUT THE AUTHOR

John Misto has been writing plays since 1992. His play, *The Shoe-Horn Sonata* has been reprinted nineteen times and sold more than sixty thousand copies. *The Shoe-Horn Sonata* also won the NSW Premier's Literary Award for Best Play and the Australia Remembers National Playwriting Prize.

Misto's other works include *Dark Voyager* about the turbulent relationship between Joan Crawford and Marilyn Monroe. Misto also wrote the hugely successful play, *Harp on the Willow* which won the Rodney Seaborn Award for Best Play. John Misto is co-writer of *Peace Train: The Cat Stevens Story* which has enjoyed several successful national tours of Australia.

John Misto's most recent play, *Lip Service* had a sell-out season at London's Park Theatre in 2017 (under the title Madame Rubinstein) and a successful season at Sydney's Ensemble Theatre and at the Lawler Theatre in Melbourne. *Lip Service* is to be performed in Poland, Lithuania and Israel.

John Misto is also an established scriptwriter and his telemovies and scripts have won many awards including the Queensland Premier's Literary Award, three Australian Film Institute Awards, three Australian Writers' Guild Awards and a Gold Plaque at the Chicago Television Awards.

John Misto has degrees in Arts and Law from the University of New South Wales.

Australian Premiere - Ensemble Theatre, 2014

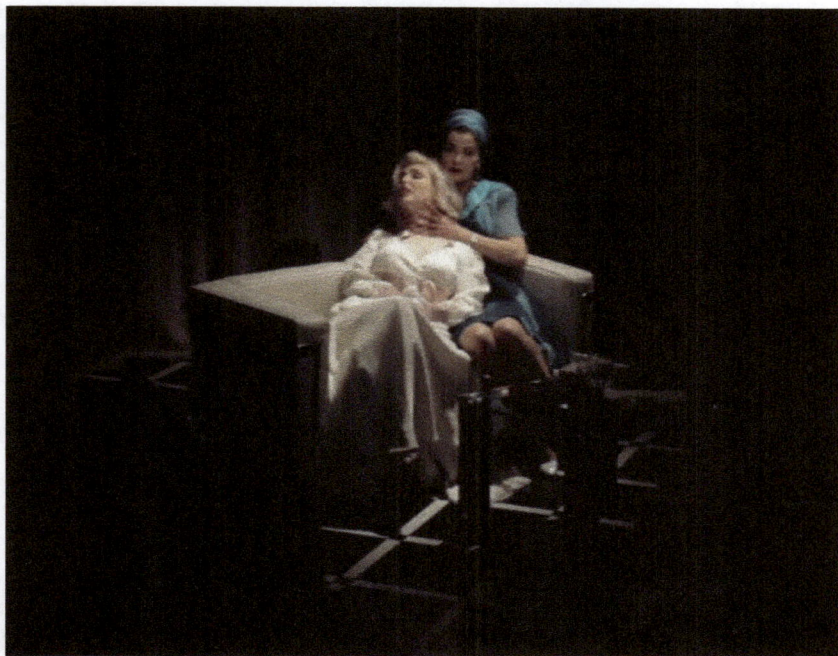

Kate Raison as Joan Crawford and Lizzie Mitchell as Marilyn in the
Ensemble Theatre production (2014) (Photo: Owen Elliott)

CHARACTERS

Bette Davis (54)   An actor experiencing a lull in her
                             career

Joan Crawford (58)   An actor experiencing a lull in her
                             career also

Hedda Hopper (70)   A failed actor who has now become
                             the most powerful columnist in the
                             United States

Marilyn Monroe (36)   An actor with problems

Skipper (24)   A WAM (Waiter-Actor-Model)

THE SETTING

Hedda Hopper's home (popularly known as *The House That Fear Built*) on 79 Tropical Drive, Beverley Hills, California, in August, 1962.

This play is inspired by real events and an actual evening that Hedda Hopper "enjoyed" with Bette Davis and Joan Crawford around the same time that Marilyn Monroe died.

ACT ONE
SCENE 1

From the darkness Doris Day sings "Pillow Talk", an energetic and coyly suggestive song about sex.

On a screen we see the following words -

"Much of what you are about to see is true - or inspired by some very delicious rumours.

79 Tropical Drive, Beverly Hills, California. August, 1962."

The lights come up to reveal the foyer and entertaining area of an elegant house.

The owner of the house, Miss Hedda Hopper, is talking into a telephone.

Hedda Hopper is an imposing, failed-actress in a colourful designer dress. She possesses the destructive energy of the truly self-righteous. The very mention of her name sends a shudder of fear throughout Hollywood, like the aftershock of an L.A. earthquake.

A Waiter in a white jacket is arranging finger food and drinks on a cocktail bar near Hedda. Like every Californian male of the 1960's, this Waiter is movie-star handsome. His tight dinner-jacket highlights his athletic figure. He is tanned and clean-cut, and although he is often mistaken for Ty Hardin or Troy Donahue, his name is Skip.

When Skip is under pressure - real pressure - he sometimes stutters very slightly - especially on any word beginning with C or K.

HEDDA: *(into the telephone)* Rock - darling - what can I say? I just adored every frame of it - those love scenes with Doris were more than I could bear!... And speaking of love scenes - a dear friend of mine has given me some photos - yes - of you - *(ominously)* - but not the kind you'd want to autograph. I said to him, "J. Edgar - these have to be fakes. Rock would never share a bathtub with two tight-enders from the Oklahoma football team."

Hedda pauses for a few seconds while Rock tries to defend himself. Hedda barely listens. She is much more interested in scrutinizing the drinking glasses for evidence of smears.

HEDDA: Yes, Rock, I know some people call him Gay Edgar Hoover – but he's not the one who's been caught playing ball with those two Oklahomos. *(reproachfully)* If my fifty million readers ever catch a glimpse of these, you'll be as popular at the box office as Gidget with the clap.

Hedda clicks her finger at Skip, then turns her back to him. Skip zips up her dress from behind. He does this calmly, with expertise, as if he has done it a hundred times before.

HEDDA: *(to Rock, with a hint of clemency)* That's exactly what I said to Hoover - you were probably sloshed and those sister-marrying hillbillies set you up... But J. Edgar's not as kind-hearted as me. He says your wedding was a sham - and sticking feathers in your butt doesn't make you a cock, Rock!... All right, all right, stop crying - I promise I'll ring Hoover and beg him not to publish them. But you owe me a favour now, Rock.

As Hedda speaks to Rock, she adjusts Skip's tie or brushes his coat.

HEDDA: *(sternly to Rock)* Is it true that Doris Day has had a secret hysterectomy?... *(irate)* No - it won't affect her voice - that's a tonsillectomy! A hysterectomy is - *(frustrated)* - oh ask your wife. And while you're at it, get her to tell you what a vagina is for. If you were any lighter in your loafers, you'd float away.

And Hedda hangs up. Then Hedda picks up a wine glass and frowns.

HEDDA: *(irate)* Look at this. Not a smudge – not a mark – they must be surgically clean. Joan can sniff out dirt like a pig hunting truffles.

SKIP: Yes, Miss Hopper.

And Hedda stops and re-folds a napkin.

Skip looks around, makes sure Hedda cannot see him. Then stands with his back to Hedda and spits into the cocktails and stirs quickly, before putting the jar in a bar fridge.

HEDDA: Skip? What are you doing?

Skip wonders if he has been caught.

HEDDA: You aren't paid to stare out windows.

SKIP: *(indicating window)* They should be here by now. No one ever keeps you waiting.

HEDDA: Stars like to be a little late - so they can make a grand entrance.

SKIP: Stars? Two has-beens like Crawford and Davis?

HEDDA: Miss Crawford - Miss Davis. You will treat them with respect.

SKIP: *(handing a pre-mixed drink to her)* Of course, Miss Hopper.

HEDDA: And don't forget to ply them with booze. They'll be as testy as albinos under a sun lamp.

SKIP: Why?

HEDDA: Don't you ever read Variety? Jack Warner's screening the rough cut from ***Baby Jane*** tonight. He told me it's the worst thing he's seen since the bombing of Pearl Harbour. No wonder Bette and Joan would rather come here than sit through their own picture.

Suddenly we can hear the hysterical voices of Women screaming off-stage -

THE FANS: (Voice Only) Joan - over here! Joan! Please!

SKIP: This might get ugly - should I bring her in?

HEDDA: Never interrupt Joan when she's feeding her fans. And no matter what happens, avoid physical violence - unless in self-defence. Understand?

SKIP: Yes, M'am.

THE FANS: (**Voice Only**) We love Joan! We love Joan!

Meanwhile Hedda begins to inspect Skip, adjusting his collar, brushing lint away.

HEDDA: The only people who can stand their company without wanting to kill them are faggots. You aren't a faggot, are you Skip?

SKIP: You know I'm not, Miss H.

HEDDA: Pity. It would have made tonight easier for you.

The doorbell rings.

HEDDA: Go on - let Joan in. And tell her I'll be down when I've finished my make-up... It's my turn to keep her waiting.

Hedda departs. Skip opens the front door and admits a small woman wearing a not-too-flattering dress and beret. She is in her early 50's and so totally nondescript that it is hard to believe this is Bette Davis.

SKIP: *(brightly)* Good evening Miss - *(stops suddenly, stares at her, then says without enthusiasm)* Oh - I thought you were Joan Crawford.

BETTE: *(striding in)* I'm sorry to disappoint you.

Skip begins to do a last minute clean-up, hardly looking at the new arrival.

SKIP: *(reproachfully)* Servants and Negroes use the back door. Miss Crawford should have taught you that. She must let her help get away with murder.

BETTE: Her help! *(grimly)* Do you know who I am?

SKIP: *(unapologetic)* Let me guess - she calls you her "personal assistant" - *(indicates a chair)* - well - go on - wipe this down so it's clean for her fat ass.

BETTE: Hedda must have been desperate when she put a bow tie on you.

Bette looks around the dining room.

BETTE: Speaking of which - where is our Medusa?

SKIP: Huh?

BETTE: Satan's daughter. Your employer.

SKIP: Upstairs - filling the cracks with Max Factor.

Bette makes a bee-line for the liquor cabinet but Skip blocks her and redirects her to another door.

SKIP: *(points)* Kitchen's that way.

BETTE: You'd banish me without a drink? I thought servants were meant to look out for each other.

SKIP: *(conspiratorially)* If you want a scotch, be quick about it. And don't touch Madam's soda water. I've just topped it up.

And Skip makes a spitting gesture.

BETTE: *(fascinated)* How refreshing to see a man so devoted to his boss.

SKIP: *(slightly defensive)* And I suppose you love Joan Crawford?

Bette laughs. It is not a joyous sound.

BETTE: *(almost accusingly)* Where do I know your face from?

Skip looks at her - hoping to be recognized.

BETTE: *(scornfully)* You probably parked my car once.

SKIP: *(proudly)* **Gunsmoke**. Episode Ninety-Three. I was Sitting Bull's long-lost nephew. I had seven words. *(re-enacting it with angry intensity and hand-gestures)* "White Eyes steal Running Dog's fire-water!"

BETTE: *(pouring herself a drink)* I should have guessed it. *(almost wearily)* You're a WAM.

SKIP: *(What's)* A WAM?

BETTE: Waiter-actor-model. Every restaurant in Hollywood's full of them. They recite what's on the menu like the soliloquy from Hamlet.

SKIP: My agent's convinced I'll make it one day.

BETTE: *(studying him)* With a profile like that? I doubt it. *(touching his cheeks)* Jelly jaws. They'll ruin you for close-ups.

Skip, unnerved, glances in the mirror.

BETTE: Cary Grant had the same problem. But he fixed it.

SKIP: *(eagerly)* How?

BETTE: By doing lots and lots of... blow-jobs.

SKIP: *(feeling his chin, suspicious)* How come you're such an expert? I'll bet you were an actress once - til the talkies arrived – and they heard your voice.

BETTE: *(irritated)* And what's wrong with my vocal instrument?

SKIP: Nothing - if you like the sound of gravel in a blender. *(accusingly)* You're a WAM too - aren't you? Waitress - actress - maid.

Skip is interrupted by excited shouts outside. Unseen Women are calling out -

WOMEN: (Voice Only) Miss Crawford! Miss Crawford!

BETTE: Ah - Joan has brought her menagerie.

SKIP: *(It)* Sounds like they're attacking her.

BETTE: Yes. The fans have hit the shit all right.

SKIP: *(looking out the window at Joan)* She'll need every fan she can get once her latest picture comes out. *(confidentially)* Jack Warner showed Hedda some "rushes". She said it's easier to stay awake under ether. Who wants to see a show about two old broads anyway?

BETTE: *(defensive)* Those "two old broads" have notched up - between them – one hundred and forty-six films and three Oscars.

SKIP: *(grins)* You forgot the eight abortions and nine husbands. They walked down the aisle so often, they wore out the carpet.

BETTE: *(not pleased)* Hedda told you that?

SKIP: I dust her memoirs from time to time.

BETTE: And what else does she say in that dirty book of hers?

SKIP: *(amused)* The only people who can stand their company without wanting to kill them are –

Skip is interrupted by Hedda's loud voice -

HEDDA: Bette!

And the force-field of charm that is Hedda rushes forth to greet her guest.

BETTE: At last - our hostess - how kind of you to make an appearance.

Hedda and Bette exchange air-kisses.

HEDDA: Have I kept you waiting, darling? I was upstairs and -

BETTE: *(finishing for her)* - and Mammy took forever pulling in your girdle.

HEDDA: *(to Skip)* Fix Miss Davis a drink. *(to Bette)* Scotch?

BETTE: Without soda... Miss Crawford will have Formaldehyde.

Skip moves off to make the drinks.

HEDDA: *(to Bette)* If you detest Joan so much, why make a movie with her?

BETTE: Because the loneliest moment in a woman's life is when she's sitting in her kitchen reading her divorce papers. I ought to know. I've done it four times. So when the studio offered me *Baby Jane*, I jumped at the chance to get back to work. Besides, it's time somebody taught Joan how to act.

More yells from outside.

HEDDA: *(concerned)* Oh dear - it's time to rescue her.

BETTE: Just send out a Saint Bernard with a Pepsi round its neck. Joan'll think it's her last husband and follow him inside.

But Hedda has already gone through the door.

Skip and Bette are alone now. Skip stares at Bette nervously. Bette calmly walks to the sofa but it is clear that she is smouldering with anger. She removes her coat, folds it neatly and then drops it calmly onto the floor.

SKIP: Miss Davis - I'm so sorry. I thought –

BETTE: If God wanted you to think, he would have given you a brain.

20

SKIP: *(picking up Bette's coat)* You look so different off the screen - and we never saw old movies in the navy.

BETTE: A sailor boy, huh?

SKIP: Did a three year stint before I landed this job.

And Skip passes the first of many drinks to Bette. Bette takes the drink, then moves one finger to the middle of the glass.

BETTE: *(showing the glass to Skip)* Well then, Popeye, take a careful look: that is my personal Plimsoll Line. If the booze level drops below here, watch out!

SKIP: Yes, M'am.

Bette looks around the room, appraising it.

BETTE: So this is Hedda's lair.

SKIP: She calls it The House That Fear Built. *(anxiously)* You won't tell her about my mistake?

Bette does not appear to have heard Skip. Instead she picks up a vase and ashes her cigarette in it.

SKIP: *(nervously)* Miss Davis - please - she doesn't like anyone touching that.

BETTE: *(examining the vase with admiration)* Tiffany's... hmmm... I'll bet it's an original.

Then Bette tosses the vase in the air -

SKIP: No!

But Skip catches it by diving through the air and landing on the floor with the vase in his hands.

SKIP: Sweet snivelling Jesus! Do you want her to bite my balls off?

BETTE: I'll keep your secret if you keep mine.

SKIP: What secret?

And Bette calmly scratches the side of the vase with her cigarette lighter. Skip, who is still kneeling on the floor, re-acts in horror.

SKIP: No... no... no...

Bette holds the vase up, ready to smash it on Skip's head.

BETTE: *(grimly)* Now tell me the truth. *(accusingly)* You recognised me when you opened that door, didn't you?

SKIP: I'm terribly sorry. I should have looked closer.

BETTE: My face is better known than the Mona Lisa's. Did Hedda put you up to this?

SKIP: I didn't know you. Honest. I always thought a movie star would look a lot like –

BETTE: Like?

SKIP: That.

And Skip indicates the doorway where a very slim, elegant Joan Crawford is standing, clutching a bottle of Pepsi in her outstretched arm.

Joan's outfit is stylish, soignée and flattering - although her shoulder pads might be a little overdone. But Skip is correct - she looks like a star.

Outside frantic cries of "We love you Joan" and "Please don't leave us" can be heard from her Adoring Fans as well as the blinding lights of flashbulbs popping.

JOAN: *(blowing kisses to her unseen fans outside)* God bless you for such kindness.

HEDDA: *(to Joan)* Are you sure you're OK? They were scaring me out there.

JOAN: *(who has enjoyed every second)* They scare me too - all that unrestrained love - but what can I do?

BETTE: *(calmly)* You could stop paying them to follow you around.

HEDDA: *(tactfully)* Bette's in a... playful mood tonight.

JOAN: *(sweetly)* It's just her way of expressing affection.

As Joan and Bette exchange very frigid air-kisses -

JOAN: This darling woman is the older sister I've always wanted.

BETTE: *(sweetly)* Young Joan's talent is truly sensational. Why she carries our movie - on her very broad shoulders.

23

Joan suddenly notices Skip. And she's impressed

JOAN: And whose leading man is this?

SKIP: I'm -

BETTE: Oh that's just Sitting Bull.

JOAN: *(trying to remember where she has seen him)* Were you ever in one of my films?

SKIP: No, M'am.

JOAN: What a pity.

HEDDA: *(to Skip)* Pour Miss Crawford a drink. *(to Joan)* Vodka is it?

BETTE: Joan only drinks Pepsi.

SKIP: *(puzzled)* At dinner?

JOAN: *(calmly to Bette)* Stop confusing this poor waiter. *(to Skip)* My late husband - Alfred Steele - was the manager of Pepsi. No - goddamn it - he was Pepsi -

BETTE: He even looked like the bottle - short and stubby.

HEDDA: You know how sorry we all were about him.

BETTE: *(raising her glass)* Hear! Hear! To dead husbands - of whom you cannot have too many.

JOAN: *(almost tearful)* When Alfred died, Pepsi adopted me. They even asked me to sit on the board.

BETTE: *(mutters)* Really? Normally you do your best work lying down.

A telephone rings off-stage.

HEDDA: *(to Skip)* Answer it, Skipper. And tell them I'm out.

SKIP: *(as he exits)* Yes, M'am.

HEDDA: *(to Joan and Bette)* Now... my readers are desperate to hear about your movie. Who gets top billing?

BETTE: *(archly)* We are still discussing that.

JOAN: *(sweetly)* I really should give it to Bette. So many of her fans wouldn't recognise her now - while I haven't gone up a dress size since 1930.

BETTE: *(sweetly)* She's right. Our costume designer constantly says "Joan's waist is as tiny as her I.Q."

And Skip returns.

SKIP: *(discreetly)* Miss Hopper -

HEDDA: I told you - no interruptions!

SKIP: It's him.

HEDDA: Oh...*(brightly to Joan & Bette)* Then you must excuse me. I'll leave you in Skip's more-than-capable hands.

And Hedda exits.

JOAN: *(angrily to Bette)* I thought we agreed to be civil to each other!

BETTE: You can't lock up a dog with a flea and expect it not to scratch.

JOAN: Especially when the dog's a bitch.

Bette is about to give Joan a thump but Skip intervenes quickly and tactfully.

SKIP: *(to Bette)* Your Plimsoll Line's showing.

And Skip fills Bette's glass, then Joan's.

BETTE: *(to Joan)* Why did Hedda invite us here? She must be up to something.

JOAN: Maybe she wants to promote our film.

BETTE: *Baby Jane* is a celluloid abortion.

JOAN: But Hedda doesn't know that.

BETTE: All Hollywood knows it. *(to Skip)* Isn't that right?

SKIP: It's not my business to repeat Miss Hopper's -

Suddenly Joan grabs Skip by his shirt collar and yanks him upwards with terrifying ferocity.

JOAN: *(fiercely)* What's Hedda telling people about me in *Baby Jane*?

26

SKIP: *(gasping)* She said your falsies make your boobs look like the Hollywood Hills in an earthquake.

BETTE: *(triumphantly)* Hah!

JOAN: *(to Skip, indicating Bette)* And her?

SKIP: She looks like a painted whore who couldn't get screwed in Alcatraz.

Joan releases Skip, turns calmly to Bette and says -

JOAN: Then why has Hedda asked us here?

Skip realises Joan has spilled some booze on his pants.

SKIP: *(to Joan, annoyed)* Look what you did!

BETTE: *(sternly to Joan)* Is that any way to treat the star of **Gunsmoke**?

JOAN: *(puzzled by this non-sequitur)* **Gunsmoke**?

BETTE: Popeye here played a blue-eyed Apache. He had seven lines.

SKIP: *(trying to sponge the stain off his pants)* Seven words. But I turned them into lines.

BETTE: *(calmly to Joan)* Yet they never asked him back. Of course we both know why.

SKIP: *(paranoid)* Huh?

BETTE: Oh - come on. With a body like yours you should be starring in Cheyenne. You think Hedda can't see your potential?

SKIP: Wait a minute - what are you *(getting at)* -

BETTE: She's blacklisted half of Hollywood. Why should Hedda spare you?

SKIP: No - no. She's always saying how much she needs me - how she couldn't get by...*(realising)*...without me.

JOAN: *(catching on)* She calls you her "Downstairs Adonis".

BETTE: Her "hunky houseboy".

JOAN: She'll never let you leave.

BETTE: *(to Skip)* So don't waste your loyalty on Hedda. Why did she ask us here tonight?

SKIP: I'm really not sure but - *(indicating the phone extension)* Hedda's talking to Hoover – right now.

BETTE: *(surprised)* Herbert Hoover?

JOAN: J. Edgar Hoover.

BETTE: *(surprised)* They're friends?

SKIP: She calls him Jedgar.

JOAN: *(to Bette)* Where do you think she gets her gossip? I heard it from Richard Nixon's own lips.

BETTE: *(to Joan, stunned, almost speechless)* Oh my God - you're screwing Nixon?! Not even his wife will do that.

JOAN: He's the attorney for Pepsi Cola.

SKIP: If Hoover wants to ruin someone, he gets Miss Hopper to expose them in her column.

BETTE: *(with disbelief)* Don't be ridiculous. The FBI would never stoop to that.

SKIP: *(to Bette)* All week she's been discussing you - on the phone - with him. That's probably why you were summoned tonight.

BETTE: Nonsense. *(to Joan, indicating Skip)* Sitting Bullshit here couldn't lie straight in a tepee.

JOAN: *(with concern)* But my dear, what if Skipper is right? What if it's you Hoover's after?

BETTE: Me!?

JOAN: Nixon's running for Governor - and Hoover's promised to help him.

BETTE: So?

JOAN: You are the one who's been shouting at parties – *(with enthusiasm)* "Dick Nixon - before he dicks you."

BETTE: *(accusingly)* And I wonder who told him that? *(striding towards the telephone extension)* There's only one way to find out.

And Joan follows eagerly.

SKIP: No - you can't!

But Bette picks up the phone before Skip can stop her.

Bette, Joan and Skip all listen in - and we can hear the conversation -

HEDDA: (Voice Only) They'll be sloshed in another ten minutes. I'll get it out of them then.

J.EDGAR: (Voice Only) Is Crawford a dyke?

Joan flinches. Bette smiles.

HEDDA: (Voice Only) What do you think? Her shoulders are so broad by now they have to shoot her in Cinerama - just to fit them on the screen.

Bette laughs.

J.EDGAR: (Voice Only) Someone's on the line.

Skip grabs the phone and slams it down.

JOAN: *(puzzled)* J. Edgar's after both of us. What the hell have I done to the FBI?

BETTE: Hoover's just mouthing off. He gets Eczema from his panty hose.

SKIP: *(astonished)* J. Edgar Hoover wears panty hose?

BETTE: We share the same dressmaker.

JOAN: *(to Skip)* Isn't it obvious?

BETTE: He also has a passion for sequins. At FBI parties, they hang him from the ceiling and use him as a mirror ball.

JOAN: *(to Bette)* Hoover has us in the cross-hairs - we've got to do something to fix this.

BETTE: *(scornfully)* Why? If an overweight transvestite wants an all-in-brawl, then I say - "Bring it on!" *(to Skip)* Well - don't stand there like a fire hydrant waiting for a dog - Plimsoll!

And Bette holds out her glass.

JOAN: *(to Bette)* It might help if you said "please". *(to Skip)* You must forgive Miss Davis - it's a word she's never heard of.

And Hedda strides into the room.

HEDDA: *(brightly)* Here I am. Sorry about that.

BETTE: *(calmly)* About what? Calling me "a painted whore" –

JOAN: Or comparing my tits to the Hollywood Hills? What the hell is Gay Edgar up to? And why did he order you to bring us here?

HEDDA: *(innocently)* I'm just helping him with some research on the President.

BETTE: *(annoyed)* Leave Kennedy alone. The man's a saint.

HEDDA: No "saint" screws Audrey Hepburn.

31

BETTE: *(astonished)* What?!

HEDDA: *(nods)* Plus Grace Kelly - Janet Leigh - Kim Novak - and Jayne Mansfield. Even old Marlene Dietrich scored a presidential poke. He's turned the White House into a whorehouse.

JOAN: But why would Hoover ask us for assistance? I've never slept with Kennedy. It's against my religion to have sex with a Democrat.

BETTE: And I refuse to help the FBI sniff the White House bed-sheets.

HEDDA: Jedgar isn't building a dirt-file on Kennedy.

BETTE: Then what the hell is he doing?

Suddenly Hedda realises that Skip is standing in the background, listening eagerly.

HEDDA: *(to Skip)* That whisky bottle won't refill itself.

SKIP: Of course, Miss Hopper.

And Hedda waits until Skip has left the room, then -

HEDDA: It seems the Kennedys have obtained an...unfortunate photo of Jedgar.

BETTE: What sort of photo?

JOAN: *(eagerly)* Not Hoover and his boyfriend playing Doctors & Doctors?

BETTE: Or helping Santa up a chimney at Christmas?

HEDDA: It's a New Orleans mug-shot from 1931.

BETTE: *(thrilled)* Hoover was arrested?!

HEDDA: *(grimly to Bette)* One word of this to anyone and you'll end your career at Disneyland - cleaning toilets with the Seven Dwarfs.

And Bette raises her hands in mock surrender.

HEDDA: It was all a dreadful misunderstanding. Jedgar simply bent over to tie his laces - in a Louisiana Men's Room - when a plain-clothes cop just happened to –

BETTE: Oh my God- that's delicious - the drink I mean.

HEDDA: Which is why I invited my two dearest friends here.

JOAN: *(with "compassion")* Anything to help - but how?

HEDDA: Marilyn Monroe telephoned both of you from her film set last week. What did she want?

JOAN: What's that got to do with –

HEDDA: *(firmly)* What did she want?

BETTE: To talk to Joan. The switchboard made a mistake - and put her through to my dressing room.

JOAN: She just needed to say how much she admires me - for adopting my dear children. Marilyn grew up in foster care too, poor baby.

BETTE: *(to Hedda)* What do you think she was after?

HEDDA: A maternal ear - to whisper into.

JOAN: *(shrewdly)* About what?

HEDDA: Her troubles.

BETTE: Which are?

HEDDA: When JFK got bored with Marilyn, he passed her on to Bobby like a half-chewed whore-d'oeuvre. And now Bobby's ready to spit her out too. *(with false empathy)* She must be feeling very low...

JOAN: *(to Hedda)* But why ask us to mop up her tears?

HEDDA: Because the Kennedy boys like nothing more than to boast about how they crush their enemies. It gets them hard.

BETTE: And you want to know how much Bobby told Marilyn?

HEDDA: Exactly. I need to find out if his pillow-talk included his plans for Jedgar.

BETTE: *(annoyed)* You expect us to ask her that?

HEDDA: Not immediately. Befriend her first. You could ring her tomorrow and congratulate her. She's announcing her engagement - to Joe DiMaggio.

BETTE: But she's wed him once already.

HEDDA: She's taken so many pills, she can't remember who she's married.

Joan, meanwhile, is trying to hide her re-action to this news. For some reason it has pleased her.

BETTE: *(to Hedda)* And what's in all this for us?

JOAN: *(to Bette)* The satisfaction of helping one's friends.

BETTE: *(to Hedda)* Plus a glowing review of our latest film?

JOAN: *(to Hedda)* And the occasional mention – in your column - of an extremely popular soft-drink?

Hedda nods.

BETTE: *(to Hedda)* Don't you love her devotion to dear little Pepsi? *(to Joan)* One could almost believe you drink it.

JOAN: *(firmly, defensively)* Every day!

BETTE: I'm in the mood for a party game. Charades, perhaps - no - *(to Joan)* - you can't act. *(inspired)* I've got it! Blind Joan's Bluff.

HEDDA: This has nothing to do with Kennedy and Monroe.

BETTE: It has plenty. *(to Hedda)* I'll reveal what Marilyn really told me - if Joan can taste the difference between Pepsi and Coke.

JOAN: What?! Oh no - no - this time you've gone too far.

BETTE: But you drink it daily – straight from the teat.

JOAN: *(to Bette)* Of all the ugly underhanded - *(tricks you've ever played on me)*

HEDDA: *(to Joan)* Relax. Bette's joking.

BETTE: I am not this serious at funerals! I want to see if Mother Pepsi here has any taste-buds left after her years of swigging vodka.

JOAN: *(to Hedda)* You can't allow her to humiliate me.

BETTE: Of course she can. *(indicating the splendid room)* Hedda did not build this abattoir with money she made being loyal to her friends. *(to Hedda)* Think about it, Hedda. If J. Edgar sinks, you'll go down with him. Your oil-well of gossip will be all dried up.

HEDDA: *(annoyed)* And you just want to punish Joan because she steals the movie from you.

JOAN: *(touched)* Why thank you, Hedda.

BETTE: I can act her off the screen any time!

HEDDA: Oh come on, Bette. I've seen those rushes. You look like Frankenstein's mother - on a bad- hair day.

BETTE: *(stung)* This - from a butcher's daughter! You've cut the throats of cows who had more talent than you were born with.

Meanwhile Skip has returned to the room - with more alcohol.

HEDDA: I appeared in one hundred and twenty films!

BETTE: So? Any competent turkey can lay one hundred and twenty eggs. *(to Skip)* Since you never see old movies and cannot recognise their stars, you would not be familiar with Hedda's screen career.

HEDDA: Don't drag Skip into this.

BETTE: He's been in this since he opened that door. *(to Skip)* I remember when Hedda first arrived at Warner Brothers – a pathetic little ingénue with the slaughterhouse blood still wet on her feet. *(to Hedda)* You struggled along in minor roles til the studio finally dumped you.

HEDDA: Because I refused to sleep with producers!

BETTE: Because your acting was as wooden as Noah's Ark. Then you changed your name from Elda Flurry - started up a gossip column – and murdered actors with your pen - all because they were better than you!

HEDDA: You are crossing the line, Miss Davis!

BETTE: No - I'm just thanking you for the welcome - *(indicates Skip)* - he gave when he pretended not to know me.

Hedda looks at Skip - who shrugs innocently.

HEDDA: You'll regret this, Bette.

BETTE: Apparently you don't want to know what Monroe really said to me. *(to Skip)* Running Dog - fetch my buffalo skin!

SKIP: Huh?

JOAN: She wants her coat.

BETTE: *(to Skip)* Since Hedda and Joan won't play charades, I'm leaving.

But Hedda is clearly tempted to give in to Bette's "request".

HEDDA: *(to Bette)* Wait!

JOAN: Hedda - please –

HEDDA: *(to Joan)* It's just a party game, dear. I mean - telling the difference between Pepsi and Coke - how hard can it be? *(to Skip)* Bring in the Pepsi. Bring in the Coke.

JOAN: No!

HEDDA: I'm sorry, Joan *(indicating Bette)* Her turn will come. I promise you.

JOAN: *(to Hedda)* I will not stay here and let you desecrate Pepsi - the only pure part of my life. This is too cruel - even for you!

Now it's Joan who heads for the door.

HEDDA: *(persuasively to Joan)* There's nothing cruel in telling my readers how stunning you are in ***Baby Jane***. The last time I sang your praises, you won an Oscar - or have you forgotten? It's your choice, Joan. Let's make this as quick and painless as possible.

Joan stops at the door, torn by indecision. But Hedda has already read Joan's mind. Hedda passes a napkin to Skip.

HEDDA: You know what to do.

Skip approaches Joan hesitantly, carefully, and proceeds to blindfold her.

BETTE: If you re-arrange the letters of Pepsi Cola, they form a new word - Episcopal.

JOAN: *(grimly to Bette)* You'll pay for this.

Hedda turns her back on them and fills a glass. Even Bette cannot see what brand of drink is in it.

HEDDA: *(giving the glass to Skip)* Here.

Skip presses the glass into Joan's trembling hands. Joan noses the glass, as if it contained wine. Then she sips its contents tentatively.

A very tense pause follows.

JOAN: *(spitting it out, like poison)* Goddamn you! This is Coke!

HEDDA: Congratulations!

JOAN: A mother always knows her child.

BETTE: Then do it again.

JOAN: Don't you ever shut up?

BETTE: *(challenging)* It was a lucky guess.

A brief pause then -

JOAN: *(defiantly holding out the glass)* Fill it up!

While Hedda checks Joan's blindfold, Skip takes another glass and begins to fill it with Pepsi. Bette, meanwhile, moves close to Skip, winks, and fills the rest of the glass with Coke. Hedda does not see this bit of subterfuge. Then Bette hands Joan the glass that is filled with a mixture of Pepsi and Coke. Joan holds the glass with both hands - as if it were a chalice - and takes a sip. As Joan struggles to work out the taste, Bette begins to sing softly – to the tune of Makin' Whoopee -

BETTE: *(sings)*
    I ASKED MY BEAU
    AND HE AGREES
    THOSE WHO THINK YOUNG
    SAY "PEPSI, PLEASE!"

And Skip joins in -

SKIP: *(sings with her)*
    'CAUSE IT'S THE RIGHT ONE
    THE MODERN LIGHT ONE
    YOU KNOW IT'S PEPSI

HEDDA: Quiet please. Our guest is tasting.

Joan, obviously unsettled, takes another sip.

JOAN: It's... it's... Jesus Christ... it's... Pepsi

And Joan tears off her blindfold.

JOAN: *(eagerly)* Well?

BETTE: You're half-right, Joan.

JOAN: *(annoyed)* What do you mean? It either is or it isn't? *(pointing to the glass)* Is this Pepsi or is this Coke?

Bette stands in front of Joan and holds up both bottles.

BETTE: It's... Poke!

HEDDA: *(looks at Skip, puzzled)* What!

Skip shrugs innocently. It takes Joan a few seconds to realise she's been conned by Bette.

JOAN: Why you lying piece of –

And Joan hurls herself at her rival.

BETTE: *(to Joan)* Where's your sense of humour, Joan? Tied up at home with Christina?

Luckily Skip intervenes and holds Joan back, while she struggles to escape.

JOAN: *(to Bette)* You can say what you want about me, but that bottle is sacred. *(turning on Hedda)* How dare you let her do this!

HEDDA: *(accusingly)* Skipper!

SKIP: I didn't see a thing.

JOAN: The people at Pepsi worship me - as much as my own children. *(pointing accusingly at Bette)* That's what galls you, isn't it? The fact that I have succeeded in business.

BETTE: *(dismissive)* Anyone can sell a soda.

JOAN: *(with sincerity and pride)* This isn't just a soda. It's America in a bottle! Cannibals in Cameroon would rather drink Pepsi than eat human flesh; housewives in Moscow are selling their bodies for a black-market cupful of this. *(waving the Pepsi bottle)* And before she went to the electric chair, Ethel Rosenberg begged to be given a glass of kosher Pepsi.

BETTE: *(to Joan)* All right. All right. You won the bet. You can tell the difference between Pepsi and Poke.

JOAN: *(slightly appeased)* I have made this planet a happier place. Is it any wonder Richard Nixon wants to nominate me for the Senate?

HEDDA: The Senate?! But you're an actress.

JOAN: So? Why shouldn't an actress be in politics? Politicians have been in actresses for years!

BETTE: *(scornfully)* You really are screwing Dick Nixon. I always said you knew how to sleep your way to the bottom.

JOAN: I'll have you know my career is spiralling upwards!

Hedda realises that the conversation is getting a bit too heated.

HEDDA: *(to Joan, in damage control)* Let's go and powder our noses, honey... *(As Hedda tactfully leads Joan off-stage)* ...and I'll tell my readers how your beautiful skin is the result of bathing in Pepsi.

JOAN: Bless you, Hedda

Joan and Hedda exit.

Skip begins to clean up the mess.

SKIP: *(to Bette)* Was she really called Elda Flurry?

BETTE: *(nods)* "Able was I ere I saw Elda." I remember her debut - in a pathetic little musical.

SKIP: She sang?

BETTE: She rubbed her vocal chords together and produced a sound like feline flatulence.
(singing)
SHE WAS JUST A TARTAR'S DAUGHTER
WHO WAS JUST A LITTLE SMARTER
THAN A TARTAR'S DAUGHTER EVER
OUGHTA BE

SKIP: Hey - she sings that when she's drunk!

And Skip joins in.

BETTE & SKIP: *(singing very rapidly)*
SO I THOUGHT THAT FOR A STARTER
I WOULD ASK TO WEAR HER GARTER
BUT SHE SORTA MADE A MARTYR OUTTA ME
"I'M A LADY WHO EXPECTS TO BE
A GENERAL SOURCE OF ECSTASY
SO MAKE OUT ALL YOUR CHEQUES TO ME"
SAID SHE
SO I SOLD MY SOUL FOR A BARTER
TO THE DAUGHTER OF A TARTAR
WHO WAS SMARTER
THAN A TARTAR OUGHTA BE

43

Bette and Skip laugh. Bette takes advantage of the thawing in their relationship.

BETTE: Did Hedda tell you not to recognise me?

SKIP: *(nods)* She thinks you're getting too big for your boobs.

BETTE: So she lets her houseboy humiliate her guests?

SKIP: No - not humiliate - I just - tenderize them for her. I think of it as a performance piece – a chance to hone my acting skills.

BETTE: And will you "perform" for Miss Crawford?

SKIP: Why? Would you like to watch?

BETTE: *(grimly)* I'd like to dip her in honey and nail her to an ant hill.

SKIP: She really gets to you, doesn't she?

BETTE: Everyone hates Hedda.

SKIP: I meant Joan.

BETTE: *(genuinely surprised)* Joan? What on earth gives you that idea? *(defensive)* I have nothing but admiration for Miss Crawford.

SKIP: If you admire her so much, why torment her?

BETTE: Because Joan and I were born to be enemies. It's our destiny. Like Yin and Yang.

SKIP: Who are they?

BETTE: *(sighs wearily)* It means a happy equilibrium.

SKIP: Huh?

BETTE: I'm a bitch. Joan is gracious. Together we balance each other out. If I knock back a role, it's offered to her - if I date Rin Tin Tin, she'll sleep with him on principle. Wherever I go, she's a few steps behind me - always as sweet as a bottle of Pepsi and as bright as a song from *Carousel*. My shadow...Joan..

And Joan returns with Hedda.

JOAN: Such beautiful singing. I thought Marni Nixon had joined us.

BETTE: Thank you.

JOAN: *(indicates Skip)* I was talking to him.

HEDDA: *(to Bette, defusing the situation)* Perhaps it's time we had our chat. *(to Joan)* I'll leave you in Skipper's capable hands.

Hedda and Bette exit. Joan and Skip remain on stage.

JOAN: *(anxiously)* What time is it?

SKIP: 9pm.

JOAN: They'll have started by now.

SKIP: *(Started what?)*

JOAN: Screening the rough cut of ***Baby Jane*** - for its first preview audience.

Joan, meanwhile, picks up a glass and begins to clean it obsessively.

SKIP: You should be there.

JOAN: *(tormented)* Are you kidding? I've seen what the big screen can do to a woman. Every wrinkle on my face looks like the San Andreas Fault Line.

Joan takes out a small flask (of vodka) and has a quick, medicinal sip. The flask is covered in the same fabric as her dress.

SKIP: It's only a movie.

JOAN: Only a movie! You ever heard of the guillotine?

SKIP: Sure.

JOAN: Well the French believed that after the "chop", the head stayed alive for an extra eight seconds.

And, on the soundtrack we hear the terrible slicing of the guillotine followed by a thud, then the jeering and cheering roars of the revolutionaries.

JOAN: And as soon as they'd killed Marie Antoinette, they held her head up to the crowd *(holding up an imaginary head)* so the last thing she'd see was the hate-filled mob as they shook their fists and raged at her.

SKIP: Wow...

JOAN: And that's what it's like to be in a bad movie - except your head is held up for weeks on end. And there's no escape - no merciful death to deafen the shouts.
(Joan puts her hand to her throat.)
I can feel the blade coming.

Skip now begins to feel sorry for her. He touches her neck sympathetically.

SKIP: You're tighter than a slipknot… You need to relax…

Skip turns on the radio. As he turns the dial in search of an appropriate station, we hear the voice of JFK – then two seconds of Marilyn Monroe singing - and finally – some tango music. Skip then approaches Joan, taking her in his arms.

JOAN: I never picked you as the tango-type.

SKIP: I learned it in the navy. What else can you do on a submarine?

And they dance...and continue to do so as the stage lights come up to reveal the small kitchen area where Bette is talking with Hedda.

HEDDA: *(sweetly)* I admire you, Bette. It takes a lot of courage to humiliate me in front of Joan Crawford.

Hedda produces a file from the kitchen drawer and opens it.

BETTE: I just tenderised you, Hedda, so you'd know what it felt like.

HEDDA: *(calmly reading from the document)* Prone to tantrums and outbursts of violence. *(to Bette)* This really sums you up.

BETTE: Is that from one of your columns?

HEDDA: No, my dear. It's your FBI file.

BETTE: *(shocked)* There's a file *through* on me?

HEDDA: I got it from Jedgar. *(menacingly)* Some of the entries really are fascinating. *(flicking the file)* Let's see - ah yes - *(finds what she's after)* Your comments about a dear friend of mine - who saved America from Card Carrying Communists. *(reads)* "A reporter told Miss Davis that Senator Joseph McCarthy had died. When he asked her how she felt, she replied: 'You should only speak good of the dead. Joe McCarthy is dead. Good.' " *(keeps flicking)* But here's my favourite *(looking menacingly at Bette)* Monday, August 23rd, 1943.

BETTE: *(threatened)* Why are you doing this?

HEDDA: *(calmly)* Because it's time you learned who's boss around here. *(reading from the file)* Eye-witnesses saw a black limousine pull up on Hollywood Boulevard. Inside, behind attention-getting sunglasses, were Miss Bette Davis and Mr Arthur Farnsworth – husband number two. They were fighting. *(to Bette)* I thought you two were happy. What went wrong?

BETTE: Greer Fucking Garson. She took away the man I loved.

HEDDA: Farnsworth?

BETTE: My Oscar! She stole my Academy Award. I'd poured my guts into making *Now, Voyager* - there was no way I could lose. But this Limey cow - with her dreadful teeth - how could Louis B. Meyer ever let her suck him off - strides up to the podium and steals my award. *(calming down a little)* It took a long time for that bruise to heal - and on Monday August 23rd, it was still red-raw and throbbing.

HEDDA: *(looking at the file)* - when you and Mr Bette Davis drove up to the Regent Tobacco Store.

BETTE: I'd run out of Lucky Strikes. And I can't breathe air without nicotine in it. So I told - *(corrects herself)* - asked Farnsie to buy me some.

HEDDA: *(looking at the file)* He yelled that he wasn't your lapdog. He climbed out of the car -

BETTE: *(defensively)* - and then he collapsed.

HEDDA: *(snaps her finger)* Just like that?

BETTE: Yes. *(with more emphasis)* Yes!

HEDDA: *(reads accusingly from the file)* "His skull hit the kerb with a sickening crack that scared the pigeons into flight."

BETTE: No. He went down gracefully.

HEDDA: Big men do not fall gracefully. You pushed him.

BETTE: The Coroner said he died from an aneurysm.

HEDDA: How much did Jack Warner pay for that verdict?

BETTE: The Coroner cleared me.

HEDDA: But J. Edgar hasn't. And at any time he chooses, he can dig up a witness who'll swear he saw you murder Farnsworth.

BETTE: *(angrily)* I hope Hoover chokes on his dildo.

HEDDA: I'll pass-on your good wishes. And if you ever humiliate me again, I will slaughter your performance in *Baby Jane*. By the time I've finished, your drag-queen fans will stop dressing as you and start dressing as Joan. *(grimly)* Now, what did Marilyn really tell you?

At first Bette hesitates.

HEDDA: *(ominously)* There are ten thousand unemployed actresses in America. One more won't make much difference.

BETTE: Marilyn wanted me to adopt her.

HEDDA: What?

BETTE: She's asked me to be her mother - in a movie she's doing about Jean Harlow.

HEDDA: Did you accept?

BETTE: I never make a picture unless I'm the star! Vanity before sanity.

HEDDA: So you told her "No"?

BETTE: Of course. Then she remembered an old dog who was desperate for a bone and offered it to Joan..

Meanwhile, in the Dining Room, the tango continues...

JOAN: If this were a movie, you'd say something... poetic.

SKIP: *(tenderly)* As you ramble on through Life
Whatever be your goal
Keep your eye upon the doughnut
And not upon the hole.

Joan looks at Skip and realises that he is actually sincere.

JOAN: Why that's...lovely. I bet you had a girl in every port.

SKIP: No, M'am! Our captain was strict. If he caught us having a - *(hesitates out of politeness.)*

JOAN: Naughty nautical?

SKIP: He'd tell our folks that their little boy had... taken his eye off the doughnut -

JOAN: *(can't resist)* And put it on the hole!

They both laugh. Then the laughter dies and they look at each other.

JOAN: *(seductively)* Your hands feel so familiar, as if they've touched me before - all over... Have they?

SKIP: *(tenderly)* Maybe we shared a bed once.

JOAN: I knew it... I never forget a body.

They are about to kiss when Bette returns from the Kitchen.

BETTE: *(to Joan)* Don't tell me the sailor's still showing you his hornpipe.

Skip and Joan stop their dancing.

JOAN: Where's Hedda?

BETTE: In the kitchen - writing our obituaries.

JOAN: *(puzzled)* What?

BETTE: She rang the studio. Our film's a turkey.

JOAN: *(all hope is lost)* What?!

BETTE: They've been laughing all through it. At us.

JOAN: At you - for covering your face with that ridiculous chalk. At least I still look attractive.

BETTE: *(dismissive)* So does the Sphinx - and it hasn't had a fuck in two thousand years either.

JOAN: *(angrily)* Why you -

Skip intervenes, keeping Joan and Bette apart.

SKIP: Don't you two ever stop? You should be trying to save your movie, not -

JOAN: *(firmly to Skip)* Sweet-pea, you're the butler. You empty the ashtrays. You mop up the blood. You flex your muscles when the guests look bored. But you don't tell us how to play this scene. *(with quiet despair)* Nothing can save ***Baby Jane*** now.

BETTE: You'll give up? Just like that?

JOAN: Do I have a choice?

BETTE: If we work together we might persuade Hedda to urge her readers to see it.

JOAN: Work together? Us?

BETTE: *(as if quoting from the Bible)* And the MGM lion shall lie down with the lamb.

BETTE: *(to Joan)* Anyway - why are we still enemies?

JOAN: Why does a rooster crow at dawn? It's in his genes.

BETTE: But The Hundred Years War didn't last this long. Maybe it's time we buried the hatchet.

SKIP: Yes - yes - that's more like it.

BETTE: Joan?

JOAN: I want top-billing on ***Baby Jane***.

BETTE: Over my dead body.

SKIP: *(to Bette)* What does it matter? The film's a flop. It's like fighting to go first to a firing squad!

JOAN: *(to Skip)* I worked hard for the right to be called The Star - and I don't give a damn if ***Baby Jane*** is worse than ***Plan 9 From Outer Space*** – I will never give up that right. *(to Bette)* For the past thirty years you've beaten me at everything - awards, pay cheques, movie roles. So if this is to be my final film, I want to go out with a bang – not a whimper! I want my name above yours.

BETTE: *(scornfully)* Joan Crawford appearing before Bette Davis?! That's too weird even for The Twilight Zone.

SKIP: Wait - wait - what happened to your peace talks?

JOAN: *(to Skip)* They're where they belong – on the cutting-room floor. *(to Bette)* You're a gambling woman, aren't you? Let's have a wager.

BETTE: What sort of wager?

JOAN: I bet I can bring Marilyn Monroe here - right now.

BETTE: You mean at gunpoint?

JOAN: No. No - she'll come of her own volition. She'll damn well beg to see me. *(persuasive)* Hedda might rescue ***Baby Jane*** if I can serve up Marilyn to her on a platter.

BETTE: And if Marilyn's a no-show?

JOAN: Your name can overshadow mine - just like it always does.

BETTE: On all the posters as well as the film?

JOAN: Yes.

54

BETTE: What the hell? Let's play for top-billing.

JOAN: *(to Skip)* Paper! Envelope! Hurry! I have to send an invitation.

Skip finds pen, paper and envelope and hands them to Joan as -

BETTE: What magic words could you possibly write to make Monroe come running here?

JOAN: *(hiding her writing from Bette)* I never reveal a twist in the plot!

BETTE: It's finally happened. You've gone insane. Let's hope Edith Head makes you a strait-jacket with shoulder pads.

Joan puts her note in the envelope and passes the envelope to Skip.

JOAN: *(to Skip)* Now Marilyn's address is -

SKIP: *(recites)* One-twenty-three-zero-Five Helena Drive. I know it like a prayer.

JOAN: Well, what are you waiting for? Deliver that letter.

SKIP: But I can't arrive on her doorstep - uninvited.

JOAN: Why not? She has an open-bed policy.

SKIP: This isn't some horny starlet. This is Monroe. Kennedy's Monroe.

JOAN: *(glancing at her watch)* By now she'll be lonely. And wearing nothing but Channel.

Bette can tell that Skip is tempted.

BETTE: *(to Skip)* She's over-rated - believe me - her beauty is only screen-deep.

JOAN: *(almost making love to him)* I saw her naked once. Her skin was like cream - you simply had to lick it... And when Marilyn reads that, she'll do anything you want.

Skip succumbs.

SKIP: *(awed whisper)* There is a God...

JOAN: *(envious)* I want to hear all about it. Blow by blow.

SKIP: *(intoxicated by lust)* Sure thing, Miss Crawford. *(as he departs)* Blow by blow...

Hedda enters seconds after Skip has departed.

HEDDA: Where's Skipper going?

BETTE: Joan sent him on an errand.

HEDDA: *(not pleased)* Without asking me? To do what?

JOAN: *(to Hedda)* Marilyn Monroe will be joining us.

HEDDA: *(reproachfully)* Why must you always get drunk?

JOAN: I haven't been this sober since Prohibition ended.

BETTE: Joan has acquired miraculous powers. She can turn Pepsi into vodka - and make bottle-blondes appear with the snap of a finger.

JOAN: *(hurt)* I try to be kind and helpful - and all I get is humiliation.

HEDDA: Marilyn won't turn up on set for a hundred grand. *(with scorn)* You think she'll paint her mole with mascara and rush over here for you? You're a has-been Joan. Accept it.

Joan is stung by this statement of the obvious.

JOAN: You ungrateful cow. No wonder your own son hates you.

HEDDA: *(threatened)* Be careful, dear. Family's off-limits.

JOAN: Pepsi's my family - and it wasn't off-limits to you. *(calmly)* Does Jedgar know that your son, William, won't even talk to you?

BETTE: *(with enjoyment)* What?!

JOAN: *(to Hedda)* Imagine if your readers found out.

BETTE: *(to Hedda)* My dear, you're being tenderised. *(to Joan)* How could any son not want to see the mother of them all?

HEDDA: William worships me!

JOAN: That's not what Dickie Nixon told me. He said you had a falling-out over April the twentieth.

BETTE: *(working it out)* Hold on just a minute - that's... Hitler's birthday.

HEDDA: I had some friends here once – to celebrate. So what?

JOAN: *(appalled)* I suppose you all sang "Happy Birthday, Adolph".

BETTE: *(angrily)* And did you bake him a cake with six million candles?

HEDDA: Some fascists - in the thirties - helped me to get movie work. I had a son to feed. We would have starved without them... And I've been monitoring their meetings ever since. But when Bill found out, he hit the roof. He fought in the war and he's a sensitive boy. He demanded that I ditch them.

JOAN: But instead you threw a Nazi party! And it cost you your son.

And now, in the background, some Third Reich "music" can be heard.

HEDDA: Don't get all high and mighty with me! You remember what Hollywood was like back then. You either knelt at Stalin's altar or threw your lot in with The Fuhrer. (*As the music builds*) How was I to know he planned to wipe out half of Europe? I just thought he'd kill the Commies and save America the trouble. *(unashamed)* And that's what we remember on April the twentieth... Adolph... as he should have been.

And the music slowly dies out...

BETTE: Oh for God's sake, Hedda, men always disappoint. From Adolph to Zanuck, they're all the same.

JOAN: *(to Bette)* You just don't know how to get close to a man.

BETTE: *(scornfully)* And you do?

JOAN: Yes. Men have so much to offer - if you'll let them.

BETTE: So who was this marvel who made you happy - or was it a football team?

JOAN: *(annoyed)* I wasn't on the menu at the Hollywood Canteen. You've "entertained" more troops than Bob Hope.

HEDDA: *(to Joan)* You still haven't told us the name of this man.

BETTE: Clarke Gable. She screwed him for years.

JOAN: Leave Gable out of this... The man was Johnny Arnold.

HEDDA: Johnny who?

BETTE: An MGM cameraman - back in the 30's.

JOAN: I picked him up once - when I was... lonely... and broke.

HEDDA: *(trying to embarrass Joan)* And working as a... "hostess"?

BETTE: *(pretending to defend Joan)* Joan didn't charge. She just gave it away - to anyone in need. She was the Salvation Army of sex. *(to Joan)* Weren't you, dear?

JOAN: Shut up... Johnny grabbed my face - held it up to the light – then tossed me fifty bucks. He ordered me to buy steak with it.

HEDDA: *(surprised)* Steak?

BETTE: It's what cows turn into after your Daddy's killed them.

JOAN: He said: "I'm Greta Garbo's cameraman. And I swear to God, you've got her cheekbones, buried under those layers of fat. Eat nothing but steak for the next six weeks."

BETTE: It's called The Hollywood Diet.

JOAN: Six weeks later Johnny came to my door. I'd lost over forty pounds. He took one look at me and whispered - "Jesus Christ, I've done it. I've found the new Garbo." He used my name in the same breath as hers. *(fondly but close to tears)* Johnny Arnold - who could look at a whore - and see a goddess...

HEDDA: Pygmalion with meat – how touching.
(looking at her watch) Now where the hell is Marilyn? They didn't wait this long for Godot!

BETTE: It's time I went home - *(pointedly)* - with my top-billing.

HEDDA: You've had a lot to drink. Maybe Skip should take you.

BETTE: Driving's like sex. You do it better when you're drunk.

JOAN: *(firmly to Hedda)* She isn't going anywhere. *(to Bette)* You've bested me in everything - all my goddamn life - but once - just once - I deserve the chance to crush you.

BETTE: *(sympathetically)* Joan, Joan, Joan... I beat you because I'm better than you. I didn't have to eat a herd of cows to become a star. I got there because I can act. You can't drink a glass of Pepsi and look as if you like it.

This is too much for Joan, who attacks her old rival as violently as possible.

JOAN: *(as she hits or slaps Bette)* For every time you've sneered at me - *(slap)* - for all those jokes about my acting - my shoulders – Pepsi Cola!!!

BETTE: Jesus Christ! *(to Hedda)* Get her off me!

Bette retreats across the room as Joan follows in hot pursuit.

JOAN: *(enraged)* I haven't begun!

Bette manages to grab her handbag. She produces a small pistol from inside it - and points it at Joan. Joan freezes as-

BETTE: It's self-defence. I've got a witness.

HEDDA: *(looking at Joan and Bette, says in disgust)* Oh for the love of God!

JOAN: Hedda - stop her!

Hedda glances at "the gun".

HEDDA: *(to Joan, dismissive)* It's a cigarette lighter. *(to Bette, dismissive)* And put it away. *(to Joan and Bette)* Get out of here - now! You disgust me!

JOAN: But Marilyn -

HEDDA: *(scornfully)* Did you really think Monroe would show? She probably laughed at your "invitation".

JOAN: No!

HEDDA: Pour vodka on your wounds and lick them. That's how we cope at our age, Joan.

And even Joan knows when she's beaten.

JOAN: *(to Bette)* You always win. Goddamn it.

But now, off-stage, we hear the distinctive voice of Marilyn Monroe singing.

MARILYN: (Voice Only)
I STARTED THIS HEAT-WAVE
BY LETTING MY SEAT-WAVE
IN SUCH A WAY THAT
THE CUSTOMERS SAY THAT
I CERTAINLY CAN – CAN-CAN

Bette, Joan and Hedda turn towards the doorway in astonishment.

And now Marilyn appears, standing beside Skip. Marilyn is somewhat dishevelled – which makes her even sexier. She is wearing sunglasses, a headscarf, a long, lavish bath robe, make-up, Channel Number 5 and not much else.

Marilyn stops singing abruptly when she notices Hedda, Bette and Joan.

MARILYN: *(to Skip, in her famous, helpless voice)* Oooh gee -
you should have told me there'd be people. I'd have put
some panties on.

*Sudden darkness. And on the soundtrack we hear Marilyn
singing the rest of Heat-Wave.*

MARILYN: (Voice Only)
GEE MY ANATOMY
MAKES THE MERCURY
RISE TO NINETY-THREE
WE'RE HAVING A HEAT-WAVE
A TROPICAL HEAT-WAVE
THE WAY I MOVE THAT
THERMOMETER PROVES THAT
I CERTAINLY CAN – CAN-CAN

As the lights come up for -

INTERVAL

ACT TWO

*Now, on the soundtrack, we hear Debbie Reynolds singing 'Raise A Ruckus' from the 1962 hit movie **How The West Was Won**.*

The lights come up to reveal: A direct continuation from Marilyn Monroe's last spoken line in the previous scene. The cast are all positioned exactly as they were before Interval.

BETTE: *(to Marilyn)* There's no need for panties. It's an informal dinner.

HEDDA: Marilyn - dear - this is such a surprise.

But Marilyn doesn't seem to hear her – or Bette or even Joan.

SKIP: *(to Marilyn)* I suppose you've met these ladies.

Marilyn removes her sunglasses and looks at Joan, Bette and Hedda as if they are objects that have just appeared in her field of vision. Then she says to Skip -

MARILYN: *(calmly pointing at Joan)* I know the one with the big shoulders - *(pointing at Bette)* - and the one who killed her husband - *(pointing at Hedda)* - but who's the scary one next to her?

HEDDA: *(sweetly)* Don't you recognise your dear friend Hedda?

Marilyn, meanwhile, remains oblivious to the fuss.

HEDDA: Where are my manners? *(to Skip)* This woman is Hollywood royalty - pour her a drink!

SKIP: But she's a whisky away from oblivion.

BETTE: Then fetch Mary Queen of Scotch a double. *(mock-curtsey to Marilyn)* Your Majesty.

HEDDA: *(to Skip)* How did you get past her housekeeper?

JOAN: *(enjoying this)* Didn't I tell you? I have a key to Marilyn's front door. And Skipper here returned it for me.

BETTE: *(to Joan)* Like you'd return a bottle of Pepsi. But instead of a nickel, he got something cheaper.

HEDDA: Why would Marilyn give you a key?

MARILYN: *(to Joan)* Your house has changed since last time.

JOAN: This isn't my house, doll-face.

MARILYN: Well if you don't live here, who - *(does?)*

HEDDA: I do.

SKIP: *(to Marilyn)* She's Hedda Hopper. I'm Skip - her butler. But I'm really an actor. I've been in *Gunsmoke*.

HEDDA: *(to Skip)* This isn't the time to -

BETTE: *(to Marilyn)* He was Sitting Bull's long-lost dog.

SKIP: *(correcting Bette's remark)* I was Running Dog – Sitting Bull's long-lost nephew.

HEDDA: Skipper! *(Shut up.)*

MARILYN: *(sadly)* It's a terrible thing to lose a dog - when all they want to do is love you.

JOAN: *(to Bette)* Don't punish him because I won the bet.

BETTE: *(to Joan)* You would have to drag her over here, wouldn't you! *(cruelly mimics Marilyn)* "You should have told me there'd be people. I have nothing on but the radio."

Marilyn suddenly stumbles - but Skip manages to catch her.

SKIP: *(gently)* It's OK. I've got you.

BETTE: *(calls out as she holds up her glass)* Plimsoll!

MARILYN: *(admiringly touching Skip's biceps)* Oooh... Are those muscles?

SKIP: *(bashful but pleased)* I work out sometimes.

MARILYN: Me too.

Skip is now propping Marilyn up.

BETTE: Did you hear me, Skip?

MARILYN: *(delighted)* Your name is Skip! That's my favourite song. *(sings wistfully)*
WHEN I WAS A LAD AND OLD SKIP WAS A PUP
OVER HILLS AND MEADOWS WE'D STRAY
JUST A BOY AND HIS DOG
WE WERE BOTH FULL OF FUN
WE GEW UP TOGETHER THAT WAY

SKIP: That's lovely.

MARILYN: *(delighted)* You like it?

HEDDA: *(mutters)* Oh Jesus, she's no use to anyone like this. *(to Skip)* Get my amphetamines.

BETTE: *(angrily says to Skip)* For the last time - Plimsoll! Did you hear me, Shitting Dog?

SKIP: *(gently to Marilyn)* Sorry...

Skip helps Marilyn to a seat.

MARILYN: *(to Bette)* No wonder he's always getting lost - if that's how you treat him. *(looking closely at Bette)* Hey, didn't we work together once - years ago - when you were old?

Skip presents the amphetamines to Hedda. Marilyn sees the amphetamines container and grabs it eagerly.

MARILYN: Oooh- vitamins!

Marilyn pours a handful of them.

SKIP: *(to Marilyn)* You really shouldn't -

MARILYN: *(swallowing them)* They're delicious.

Marilyn reaches for the nearest beverage to wash-down the pills. And it happens to be a bottle of Pepsi.

BETTE: *(to Marilyn)* Sweetheart - never mix pills with Pepsi.

JOAN: *(offended)* Pepsi mixes with anything!

HEDDA: Marilyn - dear - I am desperate for an interview.

MARILYN: But I came to see - *(pointing to Joan)*- her.

JOAN: *(modestly to Hedda)* What can I say? It's humbling. *(to Marilyn)* Of course we'll have our girl-to-girl talk. But Hedda's the hostess. She must come first.

MARILYN: *(to Skip)* Which one's Hedda?

Skip indicates.

SKIP: *(to Hedda)* On the way over here I "briefed" Miss Monroe -

MARILYN: *(corrects him)* Marilyn.

SKIP: *(pleased at the familiarity)* Marilyn - about the so-called mug-shot of Jedgar.

HEDDA: *(irate)* Mr Hoover! And how dare you eavesdrop on my conversation! Have you no respect for privacy?!

SKIP: Someone had to warn her. She's in no state to defend herself. Anyway, the Kennedys don't have that photo.

HEDDA: What? *(indicates Marilyn)* I want to hear this from the horse's mouth.

BETTE: The horse's mouth is full of Dexedrine.

MARILYN: There is no mug-shot.

JOAN: *(sternly to Marilyn)* I know you wouldn't lie to me. But maybe - just maybe – those Kennedy boys aren't telling you the truth.

MARILYN: All they want is to scare Mr Hoover - which isn't very nice. Any man that fat who can squeeze into stilettos deserves our respect.

HEDDA: Damn it! I'd liked to have made Jedgar squirm for a while.

JOAN: You mean that's it?

BETTE: What an anti-climax! If this was a movie, I'd strangle the writer!

Skip, meanwhile, has noticed movement outside.

SKIP: There's someone in the garden.

JOAN: *(looking)* Oh, dear. My fans are so loyal. They'd wait for me outside an igloo. *(generously)* I'll let them see me one more time - but they'll have to be content with that.

MARILYN: *(to Joan, with concern)* You aren't going?

JOAN: I'll be back, my dear.

HEDDA: And I have a phone call to make.

JOAN: *(to Hedda, softly)* Don't forget to tell J. Edgar that I was the one who brought her here.

Joan, of course, is referring to Marilyn.

JOAN: *(sweetly to Bette)* Would you like to come out and meet my worshippers. I'll remind them who you were.

BETTE: I'd rather eat my eyeballs from a toothpick.

Hedda moves upstairs. Joan scoops up her bottle of Pepsi and heads outside. Bette remains with Skip and Marilyn.

BETTE: *(to Marilyn)* Now why did you come running here to see Mother Pepsi?

MARILYN: It's... personal.

BETTE: Nothing in your life is personal. Every dark corner has already been lit by some reporter's flashbulb. What sword is Joan holding over your head?

Instead of replying, Marilyn resumes her singing.

MARILYN: *(sings)*
I REMEMBER THE NIGHT
AT THE OLD SWIMMING HOLE
WHEN SKIP FOUND -

BETTE: The goddamn dog's called Shep - not Skip!

Skip, meanwhile, comes to Marilyn's defence by standing beside her and singing at Bette defiantly -

SKIP: *(sings)*
BUT SKIP WAS RIGHT THERE
TO THE RESCUE HE CAME

Marilyn appreciates this gesture. And she shows her gratitude by joining in -

SKIP & MARILYN: *(singing)*
HE JUMPED IN AND HELPED PULL ME OUT

As Bette exits in disgust.

MARILYN: What's her problem! Some old people should be drowned at birth!

SKIP: Don't worry. I've got your back.

MARILYN: *(touched)* That's just what Monty Clift says...

SKIP: *(impressed)* Montgomery Clift? The actor?

MARILYN: You like him?

SKIP: He's my idol.

MARILYN: Hey! Why don't I introduce you?

SKIP: *(thrilled)* Really?

MARILYN: You have so much in common. He's a fairy too.

SKIP: What? Miss Monroe - you don't understand - I'm a red-blooded -

MARILYN: Homosexual. I know. *(sadly)* All the good men are. Even Jimmy Dean. *(taking a cigarette)* He used to make me stub Lucky Strikes out on his chest. He said it saved him cleaning ashtrays. *(holding out her cigarette, ready to burn Skip)* Do you want me to -?

SKIP: No! I like women. I love women.

MARILYN: *(not believing him)* Of course you do... Hey, I'm cool with queers.

SKIP: But you've got it all wrong.

MARILYN: *(calmly)* Tonight - when you found me - I was totally naked, wasn't I?

SKIP: Absolutely.

MARILYN: And I didn't say "No"?

SKIP: You surely did not.

MARILYN: But you just... stood there and did nothing. You say you like women - *(with a little shimmy)*- well the last time I looked, I'm pretty sure that I was one.

SKIP: Even your toe-nails have curves.

MARILYN: *(oddly vulnerable)* But you kept your control.

SKIP: You looked so helpless, it just didn't seem right.

MARILYN: But when men see this, they forget what's right. *(As Marilyn speaks, she opens her gown to display her nakedness to Skip. The audience sees nothing.)* I make them forget. It's the only thing I'm good at.

SKIP: *(gasps)* Jesus Tap-Dancing Christ.

MARILYN: *(not vain, just unnerved)* You're the first man who's ever been able to resist this. It's really quite disturbing.

SKIP: *(sincerely)* Everything about you is gorgeous, Miss Monroe.

MARILYN: It was - until tonight. If you were able to keep your control, then other men will too. *(inspecting herself in the mirror)* Do you know what that means? It means the butterfly is turning into a caterpillar.

Marilyn stands in front of a mirror, examining her face, her neck, searching for signs of decay.

SKIP: *(trying to reassure her)* Miss Monroe -

MARILYN: Before you know it I'll be just like them - with shoulders like a wrestler and a scratchy voice yelling "Plimsoll! Plimsoll!" - whatever that is.

SKIP: Please don't look sad.

MARILYN: Oh I'm not sad. I'm just not allowed to smile. The studio says I show too much gum - which isn't attractive. And if you're not attractive, nobody loves you.

SKIP: *(sincerely)* I should have ravaged you, I'm sorry.

MARILYN: *(forgiving)* We all make mistakes, Shep.

SKIP: Skip. I'm Skip.

MARILYN: But now it's started, there's no going back...

Marilyn raises her arm, feels her triceps muscle – imagines that its shaking a little – and squeals in horror.

MARILYN: Did you see that? It wobbled! I'll never be able to wave again.

SKIP: *(despairing)* All right - all right - I'm queer!

MARILYN: *(immediately cheered)* Really? See - I told you so. I respect you for being so truthful.

Marilyn kisses a very confused Skip.

SKIP: I need to get drunk...

Skip exits with a bottle of booze - just as Bette returns.

BETTE: *(to Marilyn, with unexpected charm)* My mouth behaves terribly sometimes. They will never carve Famous For Her Tact on my tomb. *(gently)* But I hate watching Princess Pepsi pushing you around. Why don't you just tell her to get lost?

MARILYN: Because I'm not tough like you.

BETTE: My dear, I'm all marshmallow. We're really so alike, I could almost be your mother.

MARILYN: I hope not. My mother has a faulty brain. She doesn't even know me.

BETTE: *(with irony)* Mine was responsible for all my success. Do you want to know how she did it?

MARILYN: Not really.

BETTE: When I was ten years old, we spent Christmas in a flop house.

Now - on the soundtrack - we hear a Christmas Carol –
something melancholy - like "The Little Drummer Boy" or
"What Child Is This"

BETTE: We had no money for a tree or presents. So mother dressed me as an angel instead. We were huddled by the fire roasting chestnuts when -

MARILYN: Where was your father?

BETTE: What are you? A script editor?

MARILYN: They always leave out fathers.

BETTE: Because fathers are never there! *(distracted by the emotion of the memory)* Cut! Cut! I've forgotten my lines. Where was I?

MARILYN: By the fire - roasting clichés.

BETTE: Ah yes. One tiny spark was all it took - to graze my halo - and set my face ablaze. By the time they put the fire out, those flames had seared my eyelids shut.

MARILYN: I hope Santa brought a doctor.

BETTE: The local doctor could not be found. He was either drunk – or at Midnight Mass – or both. He arrived next morning – almost sober. *(indicating her eyes)* Mother held me down – while he ripped the skin away with tweezers.

MARILYN: *(sympathetically)* Oooh. That must have hurt more than a leg wax.

BETTE: The itching was worse. Mother tied my hands to the bed every night – to stop me from clawing at my eyes.

MARILYN: Christmas stories are meant to be happy.

BETTE: Everyone's a critic! The burning was a Christmas gift – although I didn't know it til I made my first movie. When the camera moved in for my close-up, it transformed these *(indicates her famous eyes)* - into two huge saucers that erupted on the screen. Any woman can be pretty - but thanks to mother's carelessness, I became unique.

MARILYN: What about your father? Did he ever come back?

BETTE: Once. *(calmly)* Years later, when I was famous, he appeared on my doorstep – to tell me how ashamed he was of... the career that I had chosen... And that was it. I never saw him again.
(sings sadly)
I'VE WRITTEN A LETTER TO DADDY
HIS ADDRESS IS HEAVEN ABOVE
I'VE WRITTEN, "DEAR DADDY WE MISS YOU
AND WISH YOU WERE WITH US TO LOVE"

Marilyn joins in -

BETTE & MARILYN: *(singing sadly)*
INSTEAD OF A STAMP I'VE PUT KISSES
THE POSTMAN SAYS THAT'S BEST TO DO
I'VE WRITTEN A LETTER TO DADDY
SAYING, "I LOVE YOU."

Marilyn staggers back to the sofa as Hedda strides into the room.

BETTE: *(to Hedda)* How did Hoover re-act to your wonderful news? Is he naming the next electric chair after you?

HEDDA: *(indicates Marilyn)* When I told him she was here, he hit the roof. I could hear his veins exploding on the phone. *(puzzled)* He's ordered me to take her home - at once.

BETTE: But what about his mug shot?

HEDDA: He doesn't care anymore.

BETTE: Was he drunk again?

HEDDA: Completely sober.

BETTE: Why would he want you to send her away?

HEDDA: You and Joan had better leave too.

BETTE: I am not going anywhere until I get top-billing back!

HEDDA: Jedgar says -

BETTE: *(with scorn)* Jedgar says - Jedgar says – why should you be a slave to that overweight ingrate?

HEDDA: I don't have any choice.

BETTE: Oh come on, Hedda. We all have choices. Something big is going on - and Hoover wants to keep you out of it.

HEDDA: But what could Marilyn be up to that even the FBI is scared of?

BETTE: Hitchcock would call this the Second Act Twist.

HEDDA: This isn't some Warner Brothers film script.

BETTE: Of course it's a script – Life imitates Art. Now, let's analyse the plot. Hoover knows what Marilyn's about to do because he taps her home phone.

HEDDA: But he was fine when I spoke to him earlier this evening.

BETTE: Which means before she left, she must have said something - on her phone - to send Hoover into a spin.

HEDDA: And now Jedgar doesn't want her here because - because - she's dangerous?

BETTE: *(sceptical)* Monroe? Dangerous! She could suffocate you with her peroxide fumes - but apart from that, she's a pussycat.

HEDDA: What if...What if... *(realises)* She intends to go public – about sleeping with the President? Of course - that's it - JFK's Achilles Heel is about to kick him in the groin! And Hoover's trying to distance himself from the fall-out.

BETTE: But Hoover would have told you - you're his friend.

HEDDA: I'm his tool. Walter Winchell is his friend. Hoover's saving the scoop of the century for him. And he thinks I'll take this lying down like some old dog that's lost its teeth. *(grimly)* Not this old dog and not these teeth! Marilyn's going to tell me everything first.

BETTE: Hedda - no. Make Skip put Marilyn back where he found her.

HEDDA: And let Walter Winchell grab my Pulitzer? Never!

BETTE: But you can't use her to destroy our President.

HEDDA: This is a democracy. I can destroy anyone I want!

BETTE: The Kennedy's won't let you get away with this, Hedda.

HEDDA: Have you ever seen a tornado approach? The air is so electric that you lose all sense of fear. *(calls)* Skipper!

SKIP: *(slightly intoxicated)* Yes, Miss H?

HEDDA: A tornado's on its way. No one is to leave this house.

SKIP: *(puzzled)* Which one of us is drunk?

HEDDA: *(noticing the whisky bottle Skip is holding)* Put that away. You'll be sick in the morning.

Skip sits and Bette sits beside him. Skip is still holding the bottle of whisky. Marilyn revives slightly with Skip's return.

MARILYN: *(defending him)* He needs a little comfort. He has a big announcement to make.

SKIP: I do not!

BETTE: Plimsoll!

Skip passes the whisky bottle to Bette, who has a swig from it. Marilyn says to him -

MARILYN: *(gently)* To be a good actor, you must be completely honest.

HEDDA: *(to Marilyn)* Then isn't it time you were honest with us - about you and John Kennedy?

MARILYN: No comment.

HEDDA: *(to Marilyn)* Kennedy's used you and dumped you - in front of your fans. You're entitled to revenge.

SKIP: Like John Wilkes Booth.

MARILYN: Huh?

BETTE: Another actor who destroyed a president.

SKIP: *(to Marilyn)* He shot Abraham Lincoln.

MARILYN: Oh - him. You'd never get an agent after that.

Skip exits briefly to the kitchen and returns with more alcohol.

HEDDA: *(to Marilyn)* So you don't care how much Kennedy hurt you?

MARILYN: Hurt me? We only did it once.

HEDDA: *(accusingly)* I don't believe you.

MARILYN: But I'm too "high" to lie... Jack's so nice - and he tries so hard. *(guiltily)* I guess it was all my fault. *(sadly)* Making love does nothing for me. My analyst says I'm like the sun - I give off heat - but I can't feel any. Hey - there's a word for that, isn't there?

HEDDA: Frigid.

SKIP: Ironic.

BETTE: *(to Marilyn)* Then you're not going to do a Kiss & Tell about Kennedy?

MARILYN: Are you crazy? I'm about to marry - what's-his-name.

HEDDA: Joe.

Pause. No response from Marilyn.

HEDDA: Di Maggio.

MARILYN: *(remembers)* Yes. That's the one. And he'd kill me if he ever found out.

BETTE: *(to Hedda)* So much for the story of the century. Your so-called tornado's a fart in a teacup.

HEDDA: *(to Marilyn)* Then why doesn't Hoover want you at my house? He should be on his knees thanking me for bringing you here.

MARILYN: Mr Hoover doesn't like me. He tried to dye his hair like mine - but all the skin peeled off his groin. *(almost anxiously)* Where's Joan?

SKIP: On the porch - going-down on her lipstick.

Joan strides in, elated.

JOAN: Oh - the dears - it broke their hearts to leave me... Hedda – are you all right?

HEDDA: A storm's about to break - I need to batten down the hatches.

MARILYN: It's my fault, isn't it?

HEDDA: Of course it is.

MARILYN: *(sadly)* Art brings out the worst in everyone - that's what my analyst tells me. *(realises)* Maybe I knew that all along. Maybe that's why I quit my movie.

HEDDA: *(shocked)* You've walked off ***Something's Got to Give?***!

JOAN: *(appalled)* But Fox has invested millions in that. You'll destroy an entire studio -

BETTE: *(outraged)* - if not the whole of Hollywood! How will people like us get work?

HEDDA: *(eagerly)* Does Walter Winchell know? Have you told Louella Parsons?

Marilyn shakes her head.

HEDDA: *(to Skip)* Fetch my car keys. I have to see my editor.

SKIP: Use the phone.

HEDDA: And have Hoover listen in – and pass my news on to Walter Winchell! At least now I can salvage something from this mess. *(grimly)* Nobody leaves the house – until this story's on my editor's desk.

JOAN: But it's nearly twelve.

BETTE: *(to Hedda)* Joan likes to be home by midnight. That's when she turns into a human being.

JOAN: Don't you trust us?

HEDDA: I'd trust you both to ring Louella.

JOAN: But what about Hoover's mug-shot?

BETTE: *(to Joan)* The script's just been re-written. Your sex-bomb's turned into a time bomb.

HEDDA: *(sternly to Skip)* In my absence, you're in charge of this kennel. *(indicates Bette and Joan)* So keep them here - *(pointing to the phone)* - and away from that.

Hedda, meanwhile, has opened the closet door and removed one of her trademark giant hats. She places it carefully on her head.

BETTE: *(to Hedda)* Holding us prisoners is a Federal Offence.

HEDDA: So is murdering your husband.

Hedda exits. She leaves the closet door open. Joan glances inside the closet then she exclaims in disgust.

JOAN: Wire coat-hangers!

Marilyn, meanwhile, reaches into her dressing gown pocket, removes a pill, and washes it down with alcohol.

BETTE: *(to Marilyn)* You'll kill yourself if you keep that up.

SKIP: *(wistfully)* Maybe it's for the best.

JOAN: Skipper!

SKIP: *(with longing)* You don't understand the damage she's done to men all over the world.

MARILYN: *(concerned)* But men adore me. Even Khrushchev saw The Seven Year Itch five times. That's thirty-five years of nothing but me - and he doesn't speak English.

SKIP: He doesn't need to. When you appear on a movie screen, a guy's throat gets so tight he can hardly swallow - *(indicates his groin)* - not to mention the carnage south of the border when this little soldier snaps to attention. *(in despair)* Every time a fella makes love to his wife - it's really you he's thinking of. So he can never be happy with what he's got.

JOAN: *(to Skip, impressed)* You sure know how to strip a gal naked.

MARILYN: *(puzzled)* Skipper never touched me.

JOAN: Oh, honey, he's just turned you inside out.

BETTE: *(to Marilyn)* What Skipper here's suggesting is: you've left this world a worse place than you found it.

MARILYN: *(worried)* No. That's not true.

BETTE: *(to Marilyn)* Our fans love us. We make them feel good. But you show yours a glimpse of Heaven - then slam the Pearly Gates in their faces.

Skip, meanwhile, is standing at the window.

SKIP: Two enormous men in black suits are out there.

BETTE: *(to Joan)* They sound like your lesbian fans.

JOAN: *(eagerly)* Are they reporters?

BETTE: *(to Marilyn)* They must have heard how you've just destroyed Hollywood!

SKIP: There's only one way to find out.

Skip exits. Bette studies Marilyn who in turn is staring into space, almost trance-like.

BETTE: *(thinking aloud as she looks at Marilyn)* What does Kennedy see in you?

JOAN: Have you ever known a man who could resist a helpless blonde?

MARILYN: *(defending him)* Jack's very sweet. His dog adores him.

JOAN: He's a total sham. Nixon says he's scared of being shot.

BETTE: By whom?

JOAN: The Mob - the Cubans - Jackie - take your pick. He won't visit the bathroom without a bullet proof limousine.

BETTE: Oh for heaven's sake, Joan. Leave him alone. What's JFK ever done to you?

JOAN: Nothing. And that's the trouble. He's screwed every actress in Hollywood - except for you - me - and Shirley

Temple. Why aren't we good enough to get laid in the White House?

BETTE: You were born before Kennedy's mother!

JOAN: So was Marlene Dietrich. Christ, she's old enough to have wet-nursed Hitler - and that didn't bother Jack. *(angrily)* Why her - and not me?

BETTE: *(calmly)* Well if he ever wants to hump a Sherman tank that runs on vodka, I'll let him know you're available.

JOAN: *(grimly to Bette)* You'll pay for that, Bette. Let's discuss top-billing.

BETTE: I need to powder my nose first. I'm assuming Hedda has a bathroom here. She must go someplace to wash off the blood.

JOAN: Just squat on the lawn. The dog will show you where.

BETTE: Can you be trusted alone with Marilyn?

JOAN: She'll be as safe as my own daughter.

Bette exits. Joan, meanwhile, takes a napkin from the table. She sits down on the couch and begins to tenderly clean Marilyn's make up with it.

JOAN: *(gently scolding)* You should never leave home without gloves. Didn't your mother teach you that?

MARILYN: *(drowsily)* She was too busy having electric shock-treatments. *(sadly)* She has enough volts in her brain to light the Macy's Christmas Tree. *(with urgency)* Did you bring it?

JOAN: It never leaves my side.

MARILYN: Please - I need it... *(almost pleading)* I came here - like you asked.

JOAN: *(reaching into her own blouse)* Patience, sweet-pea.

MARILYN: If I'm not wearing it tomorrow, Joe will kill me.

Joan produces a diamond ring from her blouse and slips it tenderly onto Marilyn's finger.

JOAN: Next time you remove an engagement ring - to go to bed with someone - don't forget to retrieve it afterwards.

MARILYN: I was divorced from Joe when you and I -

JOAN: *(soothingly)* Ssshhh. *(looking at the ring)* Oh, it's so pretty. *(kissing Marilyn's hand)* Those fingers were made for diamonds.

Joan casually uses the napkin to tie Marilyn's wrists together - at the front of Marilyn's body. At first Marilyn is so relieved to have her engagement ring back that she doesn't notice. Then -

MARILYN: *(curious)* What are you doing?

JOAN: *(tenderly)* Giving you a mother's love. I always secure Christina's hands before I put her into bed.

MARILYN: Why?

JOAN: So she looks like she's praying. Then I sing her favourite song. *(singing gently)*
WHEN JOHNNY COMES MARCHING HOME AGAIN
HURRAH! HURRAH!

Now Joan begins to brush Marilyn's hair. And, as she does so, she cannot resist peering down Marilyn's gown. Marilyn is just a bit too drowsy to know - or care - what's happening.

JOAN: *(singing gently)*
LET'S GIVE HIM A HEARTY WELCOME
THEN, HURRAH! HURRAH!
THE MEN WILL CHEER AND THE BOYS
WILL SHOUT
AND THE LADIES WILL ALL TURN OUT
AND WE'LL ALL FEEL GAY WHEN –

Joan slides her hand down the gown.

JOAN: *(gently but with a hint of menace)* Joe must love you very much - almost as much as I loved Gable. Did you ever go to bed with him?

MARILYN: Of course. We were married.

JOAN: I meant Gable. Clarke Gable. *(firmly)* When did you start sleeping with him?

Marilyn feels Joan's hand grow tighter. She shifts position, not seeming to realise that the discomfort is caused by Joan.

MARILYN: I'm not sure... I guess I was twelve.

JOAN: Christina knows better than to lie to me.

MARILYN: Maybe eleven then - I can't remember. Every foster home they sent me to - I took him to protect me. So whenever they pounded on the door, I could hold his photo close and -

JOAN: Who was pounding?

MARILYN: Men...The husband - the father - the uncle. Does it matter? They all wanted the same thing. And sometimes Clarke helped... and sometimes he couldn't...

JOAN: He'd still be alive if he hadn't made The Misfits. All those weeks - trapped with you - on that dry lake in Nevada.

MARILYN: It was so hot... Vultures kept circling.

JOAN: And you showed up late every day - while poor Gable - with his failing heart - sweated it out in the heat.

MARILYN: *(trying to justify her behaviour)* There were so many scenes. And the desert air dried out my memory.

JOAN: So the birds kept hovering lower and lower - they could smell Gable's death in the wind. But the biggest vulture was on the ground - and she'd already picked him clean... Do you understand how dangerous you are?

MARILYN: I can't help it.

JOAN: Of course you can't... You give off heat - just like the sun. But you can also turn it off. *(tenderly)* Would you like

89

it to be over, dear? Would you like to stop hurting the people who love you?

MARILYN: *(sleepily)* Mmmm...

Joan lowers a cushion gently onto Marilyn's face. At first Marilyn doesn't re-act. But then she begins to struggle, waving her tied hands in alarm. The smothering continues.

Just as Marilyn appears to be in real danger of dying, Bette enters and sizes up the situation at once. However Bette doesn't stop Joan. Instead, while Marilyn struggles, Bette casually pours herself a drink.

BETTE: *(calmly to Joan)* That won't help Pepsi sales, you know.

JOAN: She deserves to die after what she did to Gable.

Marilyn continues to struggle.

BETTE: *(to Joan)* As much as I'd love to see you hanged, we have a picture to promote. And I will not stand back and let you grab all the headlines!

Bette takes the cushion from Joan. Marilyn coughs and splutters while Bette unties the napkin and releases Marilyn's hands.

BETTE: *(calmly)* Are you all right? *(without waiting for a reply)* Of course you are. A stake through the heart wouldn't kill you.

MARILYN: *(unsteady)* I'm feeling a little bit... nauseous.

BETTE: *(to Marilyn, irritated)* For Christ's sake, the word is nauseated. Nauseous means you make others throw up.

JOAN: *(to Bette, not angrily)* Save your breath. Even good grammar won't help her now.

BETTE: *(calmly)* I do believe you're jealous of Marilyn.

JOAN: Of course I'm jealous. Look at her - the most idolised woman in the world - and she doesn't have the decency to enjoy it.

Now Bette and Joan sit side by side. Bette lights two cigarettes and passes one to Joan.

BETTE: *(accusingly)* Did you ever enjoy your success? *(sadly)* In the whole of my life, there was only one night that I was truly happy.

JOAN: Your first Oscar?

BETTE: *(shaking her head)* Once - in Boston - Mother ran out of money and couldn't pay our rent. We had no food - nowhere to live - but mother turned it into fun. She said "Tonight we'll have a big adventure." We packed our bags and crept down the stairs - having checked in advance which one of them creaked. *(smiles)* Those seconds in the dark – my heart in my mouth - God, I loved that - more than any film – more than any man - Mother and me - against the world... What about you? When was your shining moment?

JOAN: In 1920 - for six and a half minutes.

BETTE: You timed your first intercourse? You're more efficient than I thought.

JOAN: That's how long it takes to wash and starch a linen shirt. My mother ran a laundry. *(sadly)* She always used to say that I would never get a husband.

BETTE: *(surprised)* Why?

JOAN: *(reluctantly)* Because my shoulders were too broad - from turning the clothes-wringer day and night.

BETTE: *(with genuine sympathy)* What a bitch!

JOAN: *(sadly)* She was right... Then one day Buddy Cooper appeared and stood at that window - staring inside.

BETTE: Who was -?

JOAN: The captain of the football team. And there he was - sneering at me. I couldn't bear to look at him. So I looked down instead. And that was when I saw it – this protrusion in his trousers – as big as a family-size bottle of Pepsi.

Bette laughs and Joan smiles.

JOAN: Buddy Cooper didn't like me. He wouldn't even talk to me. But for some strange reason, Buddy Cooper wanted me. And that was when I realised... I was a fat little nothing who had something. Why do we hate each other? We have so much in common.

BETTE: *(calmly)* We have to hate each other, Joan. If we weren't at war, the world would forget us. Do you think you could live with that?

Before Joan can reply, Skip returns. He has removed his coat and tie. He is carrying a small white envelope.

SKIP: They drove off when they saw me. *(impatiently indicating the envelope)*And this telegram was on the doorstep.

Skip suddenly notices Marilyn who is now dry-retching.

SKIP: *(to Bette and Joan, but concerned about Marilyn)* What the hell happened?

JOAN: Marilyn had a nightmare.

BETTE: She dreamt that Joan was her mother.

Skip places the telegram on the drinks trolley as he hurries to help Marilyn.

BETTE: *(consolingly to Marilyn)* Try not to be sick, dear. Or you'll waste all those pills.

JOAN: *(passing the Tiffany vase to Marilyn)* Here - throw up in this.

SKIP: No!

Bette intervenes and puts her arm around Marilyn.

BETTE: *(to Joan)* I'll take care of her. *(to Marilyn)*Come with me, honey. Hedda has a latrine that's just made for your face.

Bette leads Marilyn off the stage.

SKIP: *(to Joan)* Will she be OK?

JOAN: Sure. She loves a good vomit. She learned how to do it at the Actors' Studio. *(indicating the front of the house)* What happened out there?

SKIP: *(sitting down on the sofa, exhausted)* They ran off.

JOAN: *(impressed)* Because they know a real man when they see one.

Joan stands behind Skip and begins to massage his neck.

SKIP: Miss Crawford... you shouldn't...

JOAN: Relax. It's my turn to look after you.

SKIP: Hey - that's... that's really good.

Joan, obviously enjoying this a lot, lets her hands slide lower.

JOAN: Of course its... Oh... yes... I love big shoulders...

As their dialogue continues, Skip unbuttons his shirt so that Joan can massage him properly.

JOAN: *(rubbing Skip's chest)* Where the hell do I know you from? Did we do it in my limo?

SKIP: No.

JOAN: The toilets - last year's Oscars?

SKIP: No.

JOAN: Of course - of course – Saint Patrick's Church - in the confessional booth.

SKIP: We did it at your house.

JOAN: *(stops massaging)* Are you making fun of me?

SKIP: *(pressing Joan's hands against his body)* All the walls were painted pink, with fifteen sparrows across the ceiling.

JOAN: *(astonished)* I screwed you in Christina's room?!

SKIP: *(drawing Joan closer to him)* Oh no - you didn't screw me.

JOAN: Then what exactly did I -

SKIP: *(with great intensity)* You kissed my cheek - you whispered you loved me - and told me I'd be yours forever.

JOAN: *(annoyed)* What kind of sick joke is -

SKIP: Merry - *(deliberately stutters)* Ker - Ker - Ker - Ker - Christmas.

Skip pulls Joan right against him.

SKIP: *(grimly)* Do you remember me now, Mother Dearest?

Joan looks at Skip with alarm.

Marilyn staggers into the room, supported by Bette.

MARILYN: I love that toilet. If you stick your head down far enough, you can actually hear the ocean.

Then Bette sees a shirtless Skip who looks as if he is locked in a torrid embrace with Joan.

BETTE: *(to Joan)* Jesus in Jell-O, have you no shame? Young Skip has barely crawled out of diapers.

Hedda returns. She notices the half-naked Skip.

HEDDA: *(to Skip)* What the hell are you doing?

SKIP: *(to Marilyn, Bette & Hedda)* I'd like you to meet my mother.

MARILYN: *(to Skip)* So that's where you get your broad shoulders from.

HEDDA: *(reproachfully)* Skipper!

JOAN: *(to Skip)* How dare you!

SKIP: *(to Bette & Marilyn)* Miss Crawford - Mommy Dearest - took me in when I was four. I was adopted.

MARILYN: *(calmly dropping a bombshell)* No, you weren't. You're from Montana. Joan sent you there after she had you.

SKIP: What!?

JOAN: *(trying to sound calm and genteel)* Marilyn - dear - don't be ridiculous. *(to Hedda)* She's mixing me up with Loretta Young. She had Clarke Gable's child and hid it for years.

SKIP: *(stunned, to Marilyn)* But I am from Montana.

MARILYN: *(dreamily)* Isn't that nice? Joan hasn't seen you for twenty years.

SKIP: *(to Marilyn)* How did you -

MARILYN: *(happily)* Joan told me all about you when we were in her bath...

And like a child who suddenly realises that she's revealed too much, Marilyn stops talking.

HEDDA: *(to Marilyn, smelling blood)* When you were what?

MARILYN: *(guiltily)* Nothing.

JOAN: *(trying to laugh it off)* She's deluded. Send her home.

BETTE: *(realises)* Of course - of course - *(accusingly to Joan)* That's why you have a key to her house - and why she jumps when you snap your fingers.

And the nature of Joan's relationship with Marilyn slowly dawns on Hedda.

HEDDA: *(to Bette)* You don't - you can't mean - Marilyn and Joan are -

Hedda looks at Joan and Marilyn, so shocked she has to sit down

BETTE: What do they put in Pepsi these days?

Skip stares at Joan and is suddenly overwhelmed with revulsion at what almost happened between them.

SKIP: She's my flesh and blood mother?! *(quickly doing up his shirt)* Oh God - Oh God...

MARILYN: *(concerned)* Have I said too much?

BETTE: My dear, we could listen to you all night.

SKIP: *(frustrated)* But what about me?

JOAN: No one cares about you. *(fiercely to Hedda)* Please - don't believe a word of what this over-bleached tramp is telling you.

MARILYN: *(upset)* Why is she being so mean to me? I'm just trying to be helpful.

HEDDA: *(all sympathy)* Of course you are.

MARILYN: *(to Hedda, close to tears)* She even kept my engagement ring. And my fiancé - what's-his-name - whom I love - would be so upset if he knew.

SKIP: *(to Marilyn)* What else did my mer - mer - mer - mother tell you?

MARILYN: She said your name was... Jimmy -

SKIP: Johnny.

MARILYN: That's it.

JOAN: *(lying)* Liar. Liar.

MARILYN: No. I'm telling the truth. You can ask Jack if you don't believe me.

JOAN: Jack? *(destroyed)* Dear God - the President knows about this?

MARILYN: *(digging herself in deeper)* I might have... accidentally told him.

JOAN: This can't be happening.

MARILYN: *(trying to help)* He said he'd always fancied you.

JOAN: *(a ray of hope)* Really?

MARILYN: But he could never screw a woman who'd given up her son.

Joan hurls herself at Marilyn.

JOAN: I'll kill you. I'll tear you limb from hare-brained limb!

Skip restrains Joan.

HEDDA: Joan - control yourself.

BETTE: This would make a marvellous movie.

MARILYN: Was it something I said?

HEDDA: *(angrily to Skip)* Skipper - I am truly hurt. How dare you keep this from me.

SKIP: Because I didn't want my shame to be an item of amusement in your column!

HEDDA: But I could never write about this. The studios wouldn't let me.

SKIP: *(firmly to Joan)* So who is my father?

Joan realises that she is cornered.

JOAN: *(reluctantly)* Just an "extra" - on **Gone with the Wind**. I didn't ask his name. It didn't seem important.

HEDDA: You should have had an abortion.

SKIP: Miss H!

JOAN: I was on suspension - I'd just been divorced - I thought it would stop me from getting bored.

SKIP: So why did you give me up?

JOAN: I had to. If my fans ever learned I'd had a child out of wedlock, I wouldn't get work as an usherette. So the studio found you a foster home - light-years away - in Montana. I had to wait for years before I was able to bring you home – without suspicion.

HEDDA: *(angrily to Skip)* You owed it to me to tell me, Skipper. You have bitten the claw that feeds you.

SKIP: *(indicates Joan)* I prayed *(that)* one day she'd come here. And I didn't want you to ruin our reunion.

BETTE: *(to Joan)* So what went wrong?

SKIP: *(grimly)* Tell them, Mommy Dearest. There are no secrets in this house anymore.

JOAN: *(cornered)* I did my best, goddamn you.

SKIP: Christmas Eve - we put up a tree. You said the next day you'd tell the world that you were going to adopt me. No one had ever loved me before. I was so – overwhelmed - I said - "Thank you - Mer – Mer - Mer" - but the word wouldn't come. You kissed my forehead and said so sweetly - "I cannot have a child who stutters. I'll be the laughing stock of Hollywood." Then you placed my presents on the fire - and set them all alight.

MARILYN: *(to Skip)* And that was how your face got burned.

BETTE: *(to Marilyn)* That was me, you idiot.

JOAN: *(to Skip)* Your problems with speech had nothing to do with it. Some of my best friends stutter – Jimmy Stewart - Tony Quinn -

MARILYN: Marlon Brando.

HEDDA: That's a mumble.

SKIP: *(to Bette & Marilyn)* She sent me away - on Christmas Eve.

JOAN: *(dismissively)* He was four years old. He's imagined it all.

SKIP: Two men in black suits threw me into a car! I remember it like yesterday.

HEDDA: *(sternly)* So what can you remember, Joan? Why would a mother discard her own son?

JOAN: I didn't send him back.

SKIP: Liar!

JOAN: *(with effort)* Those men were from the Mafia.

BETTE: What?

JOAN: *(reluctantly)* Who do you think ran that foster home? It costs a fortune to bury the living – *(to Skip)*- and when I brought you home, I still owed the Mob money for your board in Montana. But I was paying off three husbands - and I didn't have the cash.

BETTE: *(to Skip)* So Santa came and repossessed you.

SKIP: *(to Joan)* When they dragged me away, you didn't even protest.

JOAN: *(to Skip)* What was I supposed to do? I couldn't take on the Mafia. So what the hell are you after now?

BETTE: What do men always want? Money, of course.

SKIP: *(upset, to Joan)* No... no... I don't even want your autograph. I just want to hurt you - like you hurt me.

Skip produces a large, decorated, sponge-covered coat-hanger which he has concealed in the room.

HEDDA: Skipper!

JOAN: *(alarmed)* Don't! Please!

SKIP: *(holding up the coat-hanger)* It's padded, Mommy Dearest – so it won't leave scars.

Marilyn has crept up behind Skip and she whacks him on the head with Hedda's expensive vase.

SKIP: Oww- Oww -

Skip staggers, drops the coat-hanger and collapses on the floor.

HEDDA: *(filled with concern)* Oh no!

Hedda looks as if she is racing to assist Skip.

HEDDA: *(distraught to Marilyn)* Look what you've done!

Hedda ignores Skip. Instead she inspects the vase with great concern.

BETTE: Those Tiffany vases are lethal.

MARILYN: I guess that's why they're so expensive.

HEDDA: *(to Skip)* You son of a bitch! You've scratched it!

Hedda kicks Skip. Skip stirs, then groans.

JOAN: *(upset, to Skip)* Of all the ungrateful little brats - I'm glad I sent you back!

SKIP: *(to Marilyn)* What did you do that for? I was only going to scare her.

MARILYN: Oh. I thought if you killed her, you'd go to jail. And it would be all my fault.

SKIP: *(delighted)* I really mean that much to you?

MARILYN: Of course. I can't believe I've found someone who's even more screwed up than I am.

HEDDA: *(to Marilyn in a cautioning tone)* Don't forget you're marrying Joe again.

SKIP: You know what they say about sequels. They're never as good as the original.

BETTE: Isn't that sweet? Popeye's in love.

HEDDA: *(to Marilyn)* He'll never be any use to you, honey. He's not like that with women.

SKIP: *(shocked, to Marilyn)* Don't listen to her. It's an evil lie!

JOAN: *(appalled)* No son of mine could be a queen!

BETTE: Oh come on, Joan - you're more of a man than he'll ever be.

HEDDA: Ladies - please - I'm not implying that Skipper is queer.

BETTE: I'll bet his butt is so busy it has its own speed bumps.

HEDDA: *(to Bette)* It wasn't that busy when you last saw it.

BETTE: What?

HEDDA: *(to Joan)* You aren't the only one who fools around with "extras".

SKIP: *(to Hedda, shocked)* You can't - you don't - no one knows about that.

104

HEDDA: I know things that are hidden from God!

SKIP: Please - Miss H - I'm begging you.

HEDDA: *(to Skip)* You kept a secret from me, Skip. And now you must be punished. *(to Bette)* I was watching - from upstairs - when you first arrived tonight.

BETTE: *(irate)* To see Skip pretend not to recognise me?

HEDDA: No, my dear. To see if you recognised him.

BETTE: I've never seen Skip before in my life.

HEDDA: That's just what Joan said – and how wrong she was.

BETTE: *(fiercely but worried)* And where did our so-called meeting occur?

HEDDA: On The Boulevard, of course... After his seven word triumph sucking Sitting Bull's peace-pipe, Skip was moonlighting as a bell-boy at the Sunset Hotel.

MARILYN: *(brightly)* I love that place. I used to take my "johns" there when I was working as a - *(remembers she shouldn't talk about this part of her life)* - um - nothing...

HEDDA: *(to Bette)* You stayed there once, if memory serves.

BETTE: A lot of people stay there.

HEDDA: Jedgar bugged your room - at the Sunset Hotel.

SKIP: *(mutters)* Oh, Jesus...

BETTE: Why?!

HEDDA: He did it to protect you, dear - you'd just made a film defending Communism.

BETTE: You mean *Storm Center*? It defended freedom of speech.

HEDDA: It's the same thing. And he was worried about your state of mind.

BETTE: That son of a bitch!

JOAN: And what's this got to do with Skipper?

HEDDA: When a sweet little bell boy turned down your bed, you were very, very grateful.

JOAN: Exactly how grateful?

Skip hesitates.

JOAN: *(to Bette)* If you laid a fingernail on my son –

HEDDA: She laid more than a fingernail, Joan.

BETTE: *(to Hedda)* So I had a few drinks and felt him up - not every woman hates sex like you do.

SKIP: Please, Miss Hopper - don't.

HEDDA: *(to Skip)* It's all your fault. You're the one who provoked me.

JOAN: So what did that woman do to you, Skip?

HEDDA: Are you going to tell Joan – or shall I quote from the tape?

SKIP: Please –

HEDDA: You must learn your lesson Skip. This is the last surprise you'll spring on me.

SKIP: *(awkwardly)* I'd... never been with a woman before... And she was so - *(stutters)* Fer - fer - fer –

JOAN: Fucked up?

SKIP: Famous... I got the shakes and I...

BETTE: *(sadly)* He couldn't cut the mustard.

JOAN: *(defending her baby)* Because the mustard had mould and the jar was cracked!

SKIP: The next day I had a big audition - for a Warner Brothers movie - The FBI Story.

HEDDA: It's J. Edgar's favourite – how he crushed the Ku Klux Klan.

SKIP: He was there - and the producers too. I was desperate for that part. But just as the cameras rolled - *(points to Bette)* - she arrived. And as I started to speak, she did this with her finger.

Skip holds up his index finger - like an erection – then lets it droop.

SKIP: *(distraught)* I turned to the camera and said - "I'm not afraid of the Ker - Ker - Ker - Ku - Ker - Ker - Ker -Ker - Klux - Ker - Ker - Ker -" There was so much laughter, I couldn't finish. Then she blew me a kiss - and walked away.

JOAN: *(to Bette)* You ball-busting bitch!

Joan makes a move to hug Skip. But she can't quite bring herself to do something so maternal.

SKIP: *(angrily to Bette)* You wrecked my career - and then - tonight - you didn't even remember me.

HEDDA: Hoover found him - drunk - a few hours later. He has a soft spot for helpless young men - and he asked me to give Skip a job.

SKIP: The film of my audition did the rounds of the studios - I was laughed out of Hollywood.

MARILYN: *(to Skip)* That was you? Jack and Bobby love that film. They even screened it for the Pope.

Skip groans, sits and covers his face with his hands.

SKIP: *(to Joan)* If you'd kept me with you, I'd have been OK. You'd have found a speech therapist - and now I wouldn't stutter under st - st - stress.

MARILYN: *(tenderly to Skip)* You poor thing. I guess this explains why you didn't molest me. Your little soldier's left the army.

Skip nods.

MARILYN: *(to Skip, with a squeal of delight)* But that's wonderful! It means I'm still irresistible to men - real men.. *(kisses him)*Thank you so much for being impotent.

SKIP: I'm not impotent. I'm just a slow starter.

Suddenly - and as surprisingly as possible - one of the windows shatters when a large rock is hurled against it.

JOAN: Aaahhh!

HEDDA: What was that?

SKIP: Everyone down.

JOAN: *(to Hedda)* Call the police!

BETTE: *(to Joan)* Your fans have gone too far this time.

Hedda is already reaching for the telephone.

SKIP: *(peering outside)* It's not her fans. Those men are back.

JOAN: Who the hell are they?

SKIP: I don't know.

HEDDA: *(into the phone)* Hello? Operator? Hello?

But the phone is dead. Suddenly the lights go out. The stage now has an eerie glow, filled with shadows.

MARILYN: *(unafraid)* This is very romantic.

HEDDA: We're under attack, you over-bleached idiot.

MARILYN: Why is everyone so grumpy?

BETTE: *(to Marilyn)* Because it has to be you they've come for.

JOAN: Of course. Of course. *(with relief)* It's just a kidnap attempt. We got ourselves worked-up for nothing. The sooner we hand her over, the sooner the studio can ransom her back.

HEDDA: *(casually)* They won't pay a cent for Marilyn now. She's worth more to them dead than alive.

Hedda realises the implications of what she has just said.

HEDDA: *(shocked)* Oh my Lord... *(to Marilyn, with urgency)* Marilyn, darling, this is very important. Has the studio insured you?

MARILYN: *(nodding calmly)* My face is worth more than the whole of Alaska. *(indicates her bosom)* The twin cities – *(indicates her thighs)* Kansas – *(wriggles her toes)* Florida.

SKIP: *(to Hedda)* So why does that matter?

HEDDA: *(to Skip)* When a star walks out on a big budget picture, the studio loses a fortune. But if the star dies –and the star is insured – they can get it all back - Alaska - Florida - and the territories in between.

JOAN: *(indicates the unseen men)* No - no - Zanuck wouldn't stoop to murder.

HEDDA: This comes from higher up than Zanuck. Half the movies in this town are just excuses for money-laundering. And we all know whose behind that.

JOAN: *(not convinced)* The Mob? They wouldn't dare kill the Queen of Hollywood.

HEDDA: They'd kill the President if they had to! Now I know why Hoover backed off. Even he is scared of the Mob.

JOAN: What do we do?

HEDDA: *(indicating Marilyn)* They've come for her - so send her out. She's already destroyed more lives than Stalin. She won't add mine to the list.

SKIP: *(remembers)* Hey - maybe they sent that telegram.

HEDDA: What telegram?

SKIP: *(groping to find the telegram)* This came - tonight - for you.

HEDDA: And you're telling me now! Give me that.

Skip hands the telegram to Hedda. Hedda, who is not wearing her reading glasses, holds the telegram at arm's length so that she can read it.

HEDDA: *(disappointed)* No. It's just Jack Warner. *(reads)* Get your phone fixed, Hedda.

Hedda tosses the telegram away. Bette picks up the telegram -

BETTE: There's more. *(peering at the telegram)* **Baby Jane** preview smash-hit.

JOAN: What?! Show me!

Joan peers at the telegram. Bette now holds it at arm's length.

JOAN: *(reads)* Hollywood fag-hags give old bags-ovation. Davis & Crawford toast of the town.

BETTE: *(reads)* Oscar campaign begins tomorrow. Interview those bitches now - before they're too drunk to talk.

JOAN: We did it! We did it!

BETTE: Toast of the town!

JOAN: Oscar campaign! Thank you, Lord Jesus. I knew you'd reward all my hard work for Pepsi.

Marilyn, meanwhile, has been looking after Skip.

MARILYN: *(touching Skips' head)* Oooh - there's red stuff coming out.

HEDDA: *(to Skip)* Don't you dare bleed on my sofa! *(sternly)* Well - get the First-Aid kit.

Skip tries to stand up, but staggers.

HEDDA: Damn it - do I have to do everything myself?

Hedda exits. Joan and Bette crouch in one corner of the stage. On the other side, Marilyn tries to wrap Skip's head in a napkin.

JOAN: *(dreamily)* Imagine - another Oscar.

BETTE: Don't get your hopes up, Joan. You've had your one night stand with the Golden Boy.

JOAN: *(annoyed)* I'm damn fantastic in *Baby Jane*.

BETTE: *(sincerely)* You're absolutely brilliant.

Joan is momentarily floored by this remark.

JOAN: *(unsure if she should be offended or not)* Was that a compliment?

BETTE: *(calmly)* Yes, dear.

A puzzled pause from Joan, then –

JOAN: God, I hate it when you screw with my mind! All right, if I'm so brilliant, why won't I win?

BETTE: Because I'll probably be nominated too.

JOAN: *(sarcastically)* And you're always so much better!

BETTE: That's not the point. Our votes will cancel each other out. It happened to me on *All About Eve*. I was magic - but so was Ann Baxter. The voters were divided and –

JOAN: *(realises with dismay)* Judy Holiday won for *Born Yesterday*.

BETTE: *(bitterly)* The sardine devoured the whale... There is a solution, of course, but - no - you don't have the courage. So let's just thank our lucky stars that –

JOAN: *(taking the bait)* What don't I have the courage for?

BETTE: One final game. If you win, I won't campaign for the Oscar. I'll even tell Hedda to put that in her column.

JOAN: And if you win?

BETTE: You'll do the same. *(casually, as if it's an afterthought)* - but I'll need top-billing.

JOAN: Never!

BETTE: I can't mount an Oscar campaign unless I'm the star of the movie.

JOAN: Then you'll just have to be happy with what you've got.

BETTE: I'm never happy with what I've got. That's my goddamn problem!

BETTE: *(regaining control)* A second Oscar, Joan. Remember how good it felt the first time - wrapping your hand around hat little man's groin?

JOAN: *(tempted)* Shut up.

BETTE: Imagine your publicity photos - an Academy Award on either side - and a bottle of Pepsi in the middle.

JOAN: No way I'm falling for this. You always beat me - at everything.

BETTE: Not with men. With men we have both failed quite spectacularly. And this game of mine is all about men - well - one man in particular.

Joan looks at Bette - then realises. Skip is too pre-occupied with Marilyn to hear them.

JOAN: Your don't - you can't mean – my son.

But it's clear that Bette does.

JOAN: Haven't you done him enough harm already?

BETTE: Yes - you're right. I shouldn't have mentioned it.

A pause. Then Joan takes the bait.

JOAN: As a matter of interest – and nothing else - what's this game of yours about?

BETTE: Skipper - and you. And a mother's love.

JOAN: Go on.

BETTE: Skipper must hate you for what you did to him.

JOAN: No!

BETTE: Come on, Joan. When you let the Mob drag your son away, you destroyed his manhood. He'll never recover.

JOAN: *(annoyed)* What's this got to do with your game?

BETTE: *(baiting her)* The Mafia's back. But this time they've come for the Goddess of Love. Her next appearance will be in an open coffin. And Skip will let them take her.

JOAN: Good. No one ever confronts the Mob and lives.

BETTE: Of course but... God help you if the Press finds out your boy didn't try to save Marilyn.

Joan tries to stay calm but this prospect alarms her.

JOAN: *(firmly)* Skip takes after me! He's frightened of nothing. He'll stand by Marilyn no matter what.

BETTE: Skip's an actor. He'll hide behind the sofa with us – unless his Mommy can make him do otherwise.

JOAN: Oh my God... Is that your game? You want me to see if I can get Skip to go outside with her?

Joan points to Marilyn.

BETTE: *(nods)* If he does, you win - and I'll stand back and let you campaign for the Oscar, unopposed. But if Skip stays inside, well, I get a bite at my third statuette.

JOAN: *(shocked)* You're asking me to choose between my child and an Academy Award?!

BETTE: Children are a dime a dozen. But how many Oscars does a woman get to have?

Bette extends her hand tempting Joan to shake on the bet and seal the deal.

BETTE: *(tempting Joan)* And the Academy Award for Best Actress goes to...

The temptation proves too great for Joan. Joan slowly reaches out and shakes Bette's hand. Hedda returns with the First Aid Kit.

HEDDA: Why is she still here?

SKIP: Please, Miss H - you must let her stay.

HEDDA: Skipper - open the door for Miss Monroe. Her fans are waiting.

BETTE: Christ on a cracker, he can't even walk.

JOAN: *(to Bette)* Of course he can. *(to Skip)* Get up. Show Marilyn how strong you are!

SKIP: *(puzzled)* Huh?

HEDDA: *(to Skip)* Miss Monroe must leave us now.

JOAN: *(to Skip)* Then take her outside. The fresh air will do you good.

SKIP: *(to Hedda)* But this house is the only safe place for –

HEDDA: No where's safe with her around. They'll slaughter us all to get what they want. *(to Marilyn)* And when they've finished with us, they'll go after your Joe.

JOAN: That's ridiculous.

BETTE: Look what they did to Bugsy Siegel!

MARILYN: *(puzzled)* The rabbit?

BETTE: The gangster! They shot him sixty-one times.

MARILYN: *(alarmed)* Oh, golly - poor Joe. He hates loud noises.

Marilyn hesitates, then takes a few steps towards the door. At first Skip does not accompany her.

JOAN: *(to Marilyn, a real performance piece)* I'll go with you.

SKIP: *(surprised)* Huh?

JOAN: *(nobly)* I can't let The Mob do this again. I simply couldn't bear it. It was hard enough when they took you, Johnny.

SKIP: That upset you? Really?

JOAN: *(lying and "acting")* How could you doubt me? My little boy - those swarthy thugs. Every night - for years - I heard your screams. *(manipulative)* Which is why I want you to stay here - with Bette.

BETTE: *(suspicious)* What?

SKIP: *(puzzled, to Joan)* But you just said I should - *(go outside)*.

JOAN: I don't mind facing the Mob by myself. *(to Skip)* Now you mustn't feel... guilty – if the worst should happen. I'm used to being alone and defenceless.

Joan takes Marilyn by the arm and slowly walks to the door, praying with every step that Skip will intervene.

SKIP: *(to Joan, feeling guilty)* We could all go together. There's safety in numbers.

BETTE: *(glares at Marilyn, then says to Skipper)* You cannot risk your life for her. She won't even remember your name tomorrow.

MARILYN: *(struggling to work out what's happening)* It's Skip. Like the dog.

BETTE: *(mutters)* Bow-wow.

HEDDA: *(to Marilyn)* You cause nothing but trouble wherever you go!

MARILYN: *(upset, close to tears)* I don't understand - what did I do?

BETTE: You existed, that's what. You pouted. You squealed. You wriggled your butt. Now he seems to think those are causes worth dying for. Hell - the air-force should have dropped you on Hiroshima. I'll bet you'd have done more damage.

Suddenly a torch light - from outside the house - combs the room like a menacing searchlight. Bette, Joan, Hedda, Skip and Marilyn all dive for cover, trying desperately to hide from it.

MALE VOICE #1. Can you see anything?

MALE VOICE #2. They're in there somewhere...

Then the torch light goes out.

HEDDA: I'd better check the back door!

Hedda exits.

BETTE: *(to Skip)* In case we don't survive tonight, I need to know that you forgive me.

SKIP: *(surprised)* Sure. I guess.

JOAN: Bette, shut up!

SKIP: *(enjoying the attention)* Let her finish.

BETTE: I was wrong to make fun of... your manhood, Skip. I never dreamed it would wound you so deeply.

SKIP: I'd had a long day - and I was exhausted.

BETTE: *(with sensitivity)* We both know it was all my fault.

SKIP: *(very interested)* We do?

BETTE: I could tell you didn't find me attractive.

SKIP: But –

> *Bette puts her finger gently on Skip's lips in a "Let me finish" gesture.*

BETTE: As I felt your firm and... chiselled muscles - I realised I would never have a man like you again.

SKIP: Wow...

BETTE: *(to Skip)* Every woman dies twice – the first time is when she discovers that her looks have gone forever. I died that night, Skipper. When you looked at me and felt nothing, you killed me –

SKIP: No... no...

BETTE: Oh, you didn't mean to but...

120

SKIP: I'm so sorry. Tonight - when you arrived - I knew that you weren't one of Mother Dearest's maids. I was wrong to humiliate a Great Star like you.

JOAN: *(groans)* Oh, Christ.

BETTE: You're much too talented to throw away your career. You were riveting on *Gunsmoke*.

SKIP: *(flattered)* You saw it?

BETTE: I was glued to the screen.

SKIP: *(encouraged)* I worked really hard to make Running Dog resonate.

BETTE: If you stay in here with me, I could get the producers to bring Running Dog back.

SKIP: But Miss Kitty shot him when he tried to scalp her.

Hedda returns. She now has a baseball bat.

HEDDA: I got there just in time.

JOAN: *(persuasively to Skip)* If you send Marilyn out there - alone - you'll stutter for the rest of your life. But if you accompany me - outside - I'm certain it will cure you.

HEDDA: And what if Skipper gets hurt? Do you know how hard it is to find a houseboy who's white?

SKIP: *(to Joan) (Do)* You really think I'll stop stuttering?

JOAN: Of course. A mother knows these things. Besides, haven't you seen that film about Freud?

MARILYN: Monty Clift is in it!

JOAN: As soon as you confront your demons, you'll overcome your trauma. You have to stand up to The Mob now, Skip. You'll never get this opportunity again.

Skip takes a few tentative steps towards the door. But Bette stands in the way.)

BETTE: *(to Skip)* You'll be dumped in the Nevada desert - and coyotes will eat what the Mob leaves behind.

JOAN: *(to Skip)* Pay no attention to that child-stealing monster!

Joan is starting to look nervous. So is Skip.

BETTE: *(to Joan)* Well Joan - what are you waiting for? You keep saying Skip will be safe out there - so prove it - before that door flies off its hinges.

HEDDA: They might have guns.

BETTE: Of course they have guns. They'd be pretty lousy gangsters if they didn't. But Joan loves Skip. And she'll march out there beside him - like a true mother would – even if she dies - *(to Joan)*- won't you?

JOAN: *(cornered)* Do you even have to ask?

SKIP: *(to Joan)* All these years, I guess I've misjudged you both. *(deeply moved)* You care about me after all. *(tenderly)*

122

Thank you, Miss Davis. And thank you, Mother Dearest...
But I want you to stay.

JOAN: *(tears of relief)* Really? Oh, Skipper - Skipper - bless
you!

SKIP: Why Mother - you're crying.

Joan tenses uneasily as Skip hugs her.

SKIP: *(to Marilyn)* Let's go.

HEDDA: *(trying to stop him)* Skipper, I forbid this. If my
houseboy gets killed by the Mob, my good name will be
ruined.

Skip pushes Hedda out of the way.

SKIP: I'll never be a movie star. But at least I'll be remembered
for being Miss Monroe's last date.

SKIP: *(to Marilyn)* Keep behind me, OK?

*Marilyn takes Skip's hand, and the two of them stagger
together like two wounded soldiers towards the door.*

MARILYN: *(sings)*
WHEN JOHNNY COMES MARCHING HOME
AGAIN –

Skip joins in -

SKIP & MARILYN:
HOORAH! HOORAH!
WE'LL GIVE HIM A HEART WELCOME

THEN HOORAH! HOORAH!

JOAN: That's my boy! I'm so proud of you!

Joan, smelling victory, joins in as well.

JOAN & SKIP & MARILYN:
THE MEN WILL CHEER AND THE BOYS WILL
SHOUT
AND THE LADIES THEY WILL ALL TURN OUT
AND WE'LL ALL FEEL GAY WHEN JOHNNY
COMES –

Suddenly Bette steps deliberately on Marilyn's long dressing gown. Marilyn lurches forward and falls, bringing Skip down with her.

JOAN: Foul! Foul! That's not in the rules.

BETTE: There are no rules.

MARILYN: What did you do that for?

BETTE: He said "Keep behind me" – he used a K word – without stuttering. And he's under pressure too.

SKIP: What?!

BETTE: Freud was right. Once you made up your mind to go out there, you fixed yourself.

JOAN: No - no - he has to face them!

But Skip has already begun to test Bette's theory.

SKIP: *(slowly, tentatively)* Klan - Ku - Klux - Corny - *(proudly)* Currumbah!

BETTE: The sun has given off her heat... Skipper here is cured. I'll bet he's even a man again.

JOAN: *(to Bette)* He can't recover that fast from impotence. *(to Skip)* A goddamn crane couldn't get you up! You need to go outside.

Skip is overwhelmed and confused. There is a pounding on the door.

MARILYN: *(about to open the door)* I'll get it!

SKIP: *(dragging her away)* No!

BETTE: *(earnestly to Marilyn)* How many men will have to die before you see how lethal you are?

MARILYN: *(alarmed)* I am?

BETTE: Skipper here is dumb - and weak - but he's good - unlike everyone else in this room. *(pleading)* You must know that.

MARILYN: *(uneasily)* He has... puppy-dog eyes.

JOAN: *(seeing her victory slipping away)* No - no! They're little and dark!

BETTE: *(to Marilyn)* Could you really live with his blood on your hands - when you haven't been able to wash off Clarke Gable's?

Marilyn looks around, struggling. Then she accepts her fate.

MARILYN: *(to Skip, gently, almost tenderly)* I think you should let me... see myself out.

SKIP: But I have to go with you.

MARILYN: And ruin my big exit? No way.

Skip looks at Marilyn, overcome with gratitude. Then he kisses her hand.

SKIP: Miss Monroe - thank you...

JOAN: *(to Skip)* What if they hurt her?

MARILYN: *(bravely)* Don't be silly. Men always do what I want them to. And the day they don't - well - who wants to be a tired old actress living in the past? *(to Skip)* How do I look?

SKIP: *(sadly)* Radiant.

Marilyn puts on her sunglasses and head scarf. Then she turns to Hedda and says with polite dignity -

MARILYN: *(to Hedda)* Thank you, Joan, for a lovely evening.

JOAN: *(angrily)* I'm Joan!

MARILYN: Oh. *(to Hedda)* Well – whoever you are – good night. *(as she walks out the door alone)* Ooooh - They look like Italians. Hot-blooded types are so easy to talk to. They really don't care about words.

Marilyn opens the door, blows a kiss to Skip and departs. As she exits, we hear on the soundtrack a few lines of the real Marilyn singing her melancholy song "Bye, Bye, Baby".

Then Marilyn is gone.

Skip stands at the window, watching anxiously.

JOAN: *(shocked whisper)* No - no - no...

Bette picks up the bottle of Pepsi and says with great sincerity -

BETTE: I'd like to thank the Academy for awarding me this - my third – and most cherished - Oscar.

Skip stands at the window, trying to see Marilyn.

HEDDA: *(to Skip)* Get away from there and clean up the mess. This place looks like the Little Bighorn.

Skip does not move. He is distraught.

HEDDA: *(firmly, grimly)* Skipper?!

SKIP: It's not too late to save her.

HEDDA: It was too late the moment Marilyn walked off her film. *(grimly)* Some rules you do not break.

SKIP: I could go next door - and ring the police.

HEDDA: The Mob will find her wherever she runs. And the Coroner will have no choice but to return a verdict of Accidental Death. Now help my guests with their coats. *Reluctantly Skip opens the closet door and removes Joan's and Bette's hats and coats.*

SKIP: *(in despair)* Marilyn was right. Art brings out the worst in everyone.

HEDDA: *(persuasively)* Nonsense. Movies brighten people's lives. No one cares about the little spats that go on behind the scenes.

Suddenly we hear a woman's muffled screams. Bette, Joan and Hedda stop for one chilling second, then recover. Skip heads for the door.

HEDDA: *(firmly)* Skipper, stay where you are.

SKIP: That was her. It was Marilyn!

HEDDA: I didn't hear a thing. *(to Joan)* Did you?

JOAN: *(sadly)* Just a girl who's had too much to drink.

BETTE: *(to Joan)* It sounded like Christina to me. She must have chewed through the ropes and hit the town.

Bette and Joan get ready to depart. Skip stands at the door, longing to open it.

HEDDA: *(firmly)* Skipper, get away from there. *(tempting him)* I'm seeing Rock Hudson tomorrow. He's auditioning young actors to co-star in his next film. Why don't you join us?

Skip hesitates.

HEDDA: Do you want to meet Rock Hudson or not?

SKIP: *(sadly)* You know I do.

HEDDA: Then play by the rules.

SKIP: *(to Hedda)* Won't you ever feel guilty?

HEDDA: Elizabeth Taylor once said to me "When the sun comes up, I have morals again."

Skip reluctantly steps away from the door.

BETTE: *(to Hedda)* Another enchanted evening.

JOAN: *(to Hedda)* Which I wouldn't have missed for anything.

SKIP: *(to Joan)* Goodbye - *(stutters)* Mer- Mer - Mer –

JOAN: *(tersely)* You really should get your voice fixed.

Joan walks towards the door.

BETTE: *(almost nicely to Skip)* Good luck with your audition, Running Nose.

SKIP: *(correcting Bette)* Running Dog. *(desperately)* It's Running Dog!

But of course Bette doesn't hear him. And Skip, dismayed, sits with his head in his hands.

HEDDA: *(to Joan & Bette)* I'll see you both at the Academy Awards.

BETTE: *(sweetly)* I'm sure dear Joan can't wait to applaud me when I get my Oscar.

JOAN: Anne Bancroft is stunning in ***The Miracle Worker***. *(sweetly)* It would break my heart if Bette didn't win.

The women stand at the door and exchange air-kisses.

BETTE: *(sweetly to Joan)* Bitch!

JOAN: *(sweetly to Bette)* Cow!

HEDDA: *(sweetly to Joan & Bette)* Sluts!

Suddenly a horrifying scream off-stage. It's Marilyn being dragged to her death.

MARILYN (Voice Only): *(in terror)* Nooooooo!

Bette, Joan and Hedda turn to the audience and say brightly, in unison -

JOAN & BETTE & HEDDA: We must do lunch!

Darkness...

On a screen we see the following words -
"And the Oscar Went To -"

Now we see a photo of the real Joan Crawford smiling and holding an Academy Award.

Beneath this photo are the words
"Anne Bancroft for The Miracle Worker.
Joan Crawford gleefully accepted it on Anne Bancroft's
behalf"

Now a photograph of the real Bette Davis looking very,
very angry -and the words -

"While Bette Davis watched in fury from the wings."

<u>THE END</u>

HARP ON THE WILLOW
John Misto

John Misto's play, *Harp on the Willow*, is the incredible true story of Mary O'Hara, the internationally famous Irish singer and harpist who entered an enclosed order of nuns after the death of her husband.

When a destitute alcoholic, Kane, descends on the convent, he turns Mary's calm life into chaos. Since the nuns are not allowed to see visitors, Mary can only talk to Kane through a grille. Unaware of Mary's real identity, Kane turns her world upside down with his wildly unorthodox approach to life.

Harp is the story of their feisty relationship. It is filled with songs, drama and humour as these two unusual people transform each other's lives.

In Mary's twelve-year absence from the world, she has become a folk-music legend. Now Mary must make a choice -- to remain in the convent or return to the world.

"Beautifully written...inspirational...spiked with Misto's demonically wicked good humour." - Melbourne Stage

Casting: 2M, 3F
Full Length Play, Drama

www.origintheatrical.com.au

www.ingramcontent.com/pod-product-compliance
Lightning Source LLC
Chambersburg PA
CBHW072156090426
42740CB00012B/2295